marlisle

a new direction in knitting

Anna Maltz

Marlisle: A New Direction in Knitting
is an independent publication

First published in 2018 by Anna Maltz

Patterns and instructions, stories and schematic drawings
©Anna Maltz

Book design and pattern illustrations
©Kristin Blom

Sewn clothing
©Marilla Walker

Photography
©Elle Benton

Printed and bound in the United Kingdom
by Park Communications

A catalogue record for this book is available from the British Library.

ISBN 978-0-9955994-1-3

Digital Download Code
Thank you for buying a real paper copy of *Marlisle: A New
Direction in Knitting*. This entitles you to download one, free,
digital copy in PDF form. If you ordered your paper copy directly
from www.annamaltz.com, you will have received your personal
download code in an email. If you bought it elsewhere, you will
find your code on a sticker below. If your code is masked by a
silver sticker, use a penny to scratch off the surface and reveal
your code – as if you were playing a scratchcard lottery
(with a guaranteed win). To use your code, go directly to:
www.ravelry.com/redeem/anna-maltz-designs
enter the code and click 'Use this coupon'.

Ravelry
Download Code
MARCXSFDYRS

contents.

an introduction to marlisle.

Somewhere within the tightly bound belief that everything has been done before by someone somewhere in the world at some point in time, a little finger hole of wiggle room can usually be found to tease out a loose end and twist a different tale.

The knitting patterns and stitch structures in this book have never existed in print before, yet they are not alien, futuristic or insurmountable, and importantly, the results are easily wearable. Marlisle isn't complicated. It is stranded colourwork with a marled and textured twist. You simply work some stitches with a single yarn and others with two held together to create the patterns. By holding two noticeably different colours of yarn double in some areas, and in others separated out and worked singly or as standard stranded colourwork, you are constantly using both yarns in one way or the other — you always have whichever colour you want available to work with singly (while the other floats briefly behind). This allows patches of stranded colourwork or single-colour motifs to be scattered around a garment against a consistent background, rather than necessarily worked regularly across a round. In this way, it is straightforward to achieve effects akin to intarsia, but without needing to anchor in the patch of colour.

And that's the thing: Marlisle is a little bit like this and a little bit like that. Basically, it uses only the standard stitches of the knitting canon with minimal call for new terminology: knit and purl are used in combination with the increases and decreases needed to shape the garment. There is a handy increase you may not have encountered elsewhere that works specifically when you use two yarns held together and is, conveniently, easier to understand and work than most increases I've tried. And there's a stitch combo worthy of its own abbreviation that makes working bobbles a lot neater. The rest is so standard that it feels odd that Marlisle has not already been developed — it opens up so many interesting avenues for creating unusual, decorative texture and colour shifts in handknitted fabric with a focus on seamless knitting in the round.

Like any other approach to knitting, Marlisle has its own quirks and a lot of shared ground. Certain results have a similar look to double, shadow, mosaic or brioche knitting and can be combined successfully. By involving areas of marl, superimposed lace knitting has the most significant overlaps. Unlike all those approaches, where you have to work double the stitches or do two passes of a row, there's a WYSIWYG satisfaction to Marlisle. As with cabling, there are areas that are denser and more intensely worked than others and it can be a little complicated to

'Marlisle is a little bit like this and a little bit like that'

judge the gauge for the fabric as a whole. As with cabling, travelling stitches open up even more fun possbilities to explore. I love that Marlisle can be used to develop totally original patterns or to adapt existing designs, combine different weights of yarn and overcome frustrations such as jogging stripes when knitting in the round. It's like getting a new pair of spectacles that allow you to look at your stash with fresh eyes.

My Marlisle adventure began in 2014, when I started working on my first book, *Penguin: A Knit Collection*. With all manner of penguin species firmly on the brain, the Humboldt penguin's speckled front yet plain back got me thinking about how to achieve patches of pure white on the front only of a circular knitted, one-piece garment. Traditional stranded colourwork requires working a full round of patterning. I was keen to be able to scatter the motifs around and achieve this without working intarsia in the round, yet over distances that would be unworkable or impractical with a float of yarn behind (even if catching it). In response to these challenges, I designed the Humboldt sweater and became obsessed with the possibilities. The patterns in this book are the next steps in that exploration. I can already see where I will take it next, but I wanted to pause and share where I have gotten to so far. There's a different sort of fun to be found in experimenting when there aren't so many existing rules. We can create and discover them together as we go along, without needing to tread carefully around heritage and tradition.

'I like puns and wordplay and coined "Marlisle" as the name for this new technique. It's a made-up word mixing "marl", two different coloured strands worked together, and the "isle" from fairisle'

In so many ways, Marlisle sprang from my personal knitting preferences.

I like knitting in the round. While Marlisle is not impossible to work flat, it doesn't satisfy in quite the same way as it does in the round. Here it gives interesting solutions to a number of knitting conundrums such as jogging stripes, reversibility and how to only have patterning in certain places and not others, which have long bothered me as a knitter. And beyond knitting, Marlisle and I have more in common. I feel at home in multicultural London, where, like myself, most of my friends come from parents and/or have partners from elsewhere in the world, so ideas of knits based on pure geographic heritage feel simplistic. I grew up as the granddaughter of a weaver. When I look at these patterns and the whole concept of Marlisle, I very much see my Oma's influence: the way the colours combine is distinctly akin to weaving while retaining all the characteristics of knitting.

My family is inclined to feel cold, and while prone to Raynaud's Phenomenon alongside growing up in a medium cold weather climate, our household was one where the heat wasn't turned up if you said you were cold. Instead you were advised to put on another sweater: for economy and to avoid the environmental ramifications of the energy consumption involved in heating. Marlisle is densely knitted, making it extra warm.

I like puns and wordplay and coined 'Marlisle' as the name for this technique. It's a made-up word mixing 'marl', two different coloured strands worked together, and the 'isle' from fairisle. Fairisle used to be the catch-all term for any stranded colourwork in the UK (and a number of places beyond that too). It's amazing that a small island could lend its name to a whole technique and to me it feels rather limiting that in the quest for identification and heritage, it is now used only for knits with a strong identifying tie to the Shetland Islands.

While developing Marlisle over the past two years, I hunted through historical and contemporary knitting practices for similar methods, and had many conversations on the subject during my Marlisle workshops in Europe and America. However, I'd found only a couple of previous uses of anything vaguely resembling this technique. None of them were precisely it, until, a couple of months ago, while teaching in Copenhagen, I crossed paths with Chrissie Day, also teaching at the Knitwork.dk 2017 festival. She'd seen what I was up to as sweaterspotter on Instagram and as we chatted in the far too brief moment we had, she talked about using a similar technique. In a wonderful moment of synchronicity, she had named her approach Marltarsia, highlighting the intarsia element over the stranded colourwork 'fairisle', and had mostly used it for felting. I am sure there are other striking overlaps such as this and look forward to the discussions that discovering them will bring up. Part of the complication of tracking down references to this technique may be down to the fact that there hasn't been a name for it, which makes it hard to isolate. It feels as though it must exist, because it's so intuitive and easy to slot into existing knitting practices. Having covered it here, in this book, more concretely, I look forward to seeing where others will take this approach and hope they will do me the honour of adopting the term Marlisle, so that we can collectively see where this knitting adventure takes us.

yarn.

The yarns used in these patterns are absolutely central to how this whole book came about.

They are intrinsic to the design of the patterns themselves not just for the quality of the fibres, but also for their provenance, the people and stories that bind them and make them special to me. I grew up in 1980s London, in sweaters knitted by my mother and her mother, my Oma. Often they had also handspun the yarn, from fleeces raised by friends or friends of friends. This established for me the expectation that you could know where and whom the yarn was spun by and which sheep or flock it came from. There was so much animal and field left in those sweaters that when we visited a farm and I was let into the pen for orphaned lambs, a little, deep brown one, the same colour as my zippered cardigan, nestled in close and we were both in heaven. To me, that rusticness was very much of its time — a counterpoint to the 80s slickness and embrace of mass-production.

The 70s and 80s are interesting eras to examine, because, in many ways, they were the last gasp of DIY garments as central to the assumption of how we could dress ourselves with practicality and economy. Now we do it as a conscious act of rebellion, of subversion, as a hobby and a luxury, and with the fervour of preservation both for the skills and ourselves. The kernels of that were certainly present in previous eras, but the infrastructure was different. It is impossible to return to a time without computers and globalisation or at least hard to imagine a way where that desire is not regressive and isolating (or post-apocalyptic). I am not looking to recreate the garments of those of us who grew up then as the children of makers, farmers and hippies. Those garments still exist as heirlooms, safe in cedar chests, or being worn by the next generation of family young ones. They can be found secondhand in markets, vintage boutiques and charity shops or online via many platforms. The patterns, ready to be reknitted, can be found there too, or in libraries, or in the knitting baskets and bookshelves of those who like to hold on to things. My intention is to reimagine how we use these rustic, natural yarns, and take them somewhere new, a little unnatural.

Each of the patterns in this book is worked in a combination of a very sheepy, undyed, breed-specific yarn with clear provenance, together with a second yarn that is small-batch, hand-dyed by a specific person on a fibre blend that is pertinent to them. For this second yarn, I looked specifically at those dyers using bases that reflect their location, as well as colours that made me want to cast on straight away. It was an interesting practice to look across a range of dyers I admired and try to pick out shades that worked together in a collection, but also spoke to their specific skills and preferences. Beyond that, I wanted the two yarns to have a relationship to each other. In each pattern, you will find a yarn pairing story, explaining my motives for combining those two yarns into a project. I want to highlight how these very personal choices were made, in hopes that you will look at combining yarns with your own significances, whether they are the yarns I suggest or others that make sense to you. We can drive ourselves into a trap of wanting that thing from far away that looks so good in pictures, but finding meaning in what is accessible to us has its own joy.

More people than ever before engage in international travel for business and pleasure. And from our armchairs, desks and wherever we take a smartphone, we have unprecedented insight into the lives and tastes of others around the globe. At the same time, we are becoming more and more aware of the implications of a modern global market and mass consumption, which has led to a focus on the constant play between local and faraway.

'Local' is a stretchy term, but I far prefer it to a 'single-country-origin' which far too easily smacks of nationalism, especially when there are a number of countries that are larger than the European Union, which currently comprises 28 distinct countries. The USA is almost three times as big as the EU. Australia and Brazil are not far off the size of the USA. Russia is bigger. A single country of origin can also include territories on the other side of the globe — if you think of Britain as including the Falkland Islands (known more locally as the Islas Malvinas), they are 8,000 miles away off the coast of Argentina.

Farmer's markets often specify a 30-mile catchment area to satisfy a definition of 'local'. The inspirational Fibershed movement encourages farmers, producers, shops and consumers to form links and support each other in creating garments that can, from start to finish, be raised, made, sold and worn within a 150-mile radius in a sustainable way. If I go wild and give myself a 600-mile radius from where I live in London (which would get me from here to

Shetland or the Outer Hebrides with miles to spare), I can choose not just from British yarn, but that from 14 different countries too. London might be the centre of my world, but it isn't bang in the middle of the United Kingdom. If I were to move to Land's End in Cornwall, that would put roughly another 100 miles between me and Shetland or the Outer Hebrides. That additional mileage adds a handful of other countries to the list and becomes equivalent to considering as neighbours New York and Chicago, San Francisco and Seattle, Sydney and Adelaide, Guadalajara and Chiapas or Beijing and Shanghai. Only another 100 miles would sweep together Cape Town and Pretoria or Moscow and Yekaterinburg. The UK would fit in countries of this scale many times over, which makes the description 'made in the UK' seem comparatively local. National borders, however, quickly get complicated. The Falkland Islands produce a significant portion of wool considered British, especially Merino — but can hardly be considered as 'local' to the UK. This is where personal preference and transparency come in as a way of finding situations you feel comfortable with, based on your own standards. In this regard, I am a firm believer in nepotism. If I know the person, I know what I am reinforcing. I also know that in working together, they are also supporting me, with a clearer idea of what that means. There is trust involved that goes beyond business. That idea of mutual benefit is why you will only find this book available from small-scale, independent shops (and me). This might be a hard choice to justify if looking at it purely from a 'money-making' business angle, but I firmly believe these are the places that support knitters most when they have a problem, and I'm prepared to be more resourceful in my life in order to stick to my guns on that.

Circles of production based on proximity make sense for many reasons, not least because they bolster localised economies and reduce the many impacts of transportation. They can help maintain traditions and culture from a time before globalised consumerism and foster interesting new pockets of activity. When considering fair practices, it is easier to understand standards of work and welfare in the country in which you yourself earn a living. As consumers of yarn, we mirror a shift in consumer trends echoed elsewhere, from food to clothing: we are drawn to the story and imagery of the yarn as much as the feel of the yarn itself. This is great, because it is encouraging us to shift away from the previous decade's quest for the softest yarn, but I've noticed we like the idea of local so much that it doesn't need to be our own local. In truth, many

of the fashionable yarns we covet that are from a distinct place financially benefit someone else's neighbours, so how does that make sense in terms of proximity, and circles of production? My interest in supporting local can mean supporting someone else's local if I understand the chain of where what I use comes from, and feel engaged in it. This may seem counterintuitive, but it is also exciting: a reflection of the reality of our time and the people we are. I know I am not alone in having lived in a range of countries or having parents and partners from a different place than where I was born. My choices in yarn reflect that. Though most of the 22 different yarns I've used in this pattern collection come from the UK, from sheep raised near the yarn-producers and dyers, you will also find yarns of a similar nature from friends in Australia, Canada, France, Germany, The Netherlands, Portugal and the USA. There is also a thought-provoking yarn that involves Sweden, Germany, the UK and Argentina.

yarn substitution.

It has been a joy to work with all of these yarns and I can wholeheartedly recommend them as both perfect for each project (they were designed with them, after all) and for having interesting, creative and conscientious people behind them. However, you will and are urged to substitute yarns to reflect your personal tastes, budget constraints (and priorities), friendships and what is available where you are. By sharing the many reasons I've emotionally, aesthetically and ethically chosen each

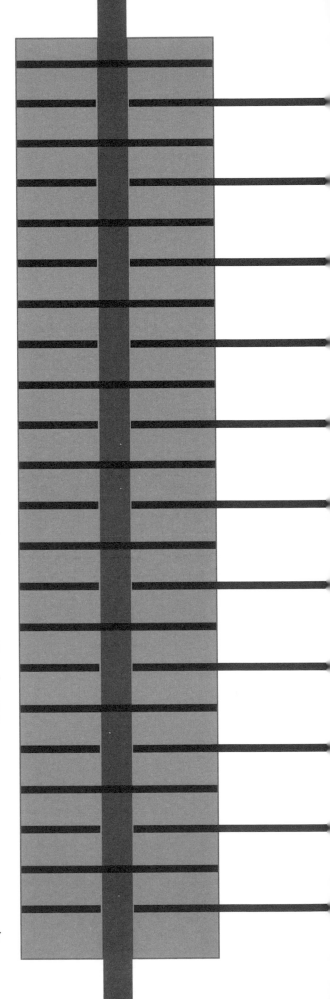

one of them, I hope to encourage you to find your own meanings in the yarn you chose, be they geographic, conceptual or otherwise.

There's a lot of advice available if you're substituting yarns. As well as looking in the obvious Yarn section of each pattern, you'll find extensive Yarn Pairing Notes that give specific details of why and how the yarns work together in regards to breed, spin type, weight, drape, etc. The two yarns you use for Marlisle need not be the same weight as each other, so it is worth thinking creatively about your yarn pairings. It's also worth cruising the Construction and Fit, Gauge and Pattern Notes sections of each pattern as suggestions and insight can also be found there. For an excellent, outside resource, www.yarnsub.com is always helpful when switching out the yarn you use. Once you have entered the specified yarn, the database gives suggestions based on similarities across a wide range of factors beyond the basic weight-to-length ratio.

stash.

The only yarns dear to me that you won't find represented in these pages are those that come from my stash. For practicality, I have listed yarns other

knitters can get their hands on. You'll find a links to all their websites in the Community Pages (page 152). This means that, at the time of going to press, both the type and colour of the recommended yarns are current for the people making them. If you want to go with an exact match (with a little leeway for the fluctuations of natural and hand-dyed), you can. I do, however, hope that you will also turn to your stash. Marlisle can shed new light on yarns you acquired ages ago. The technique offers a lovely way to reevaluate a yarn you had tucked away because it was finer than you wanted to tackle — in combo with the second yarn you'll need for Marlisle, it adds up to a heavier weight. Or maybe the colour felt like it represented a former version of yourself — Marlisle lets you combine it with something new to bring it right up to scratch.

quantity.

With Marlisle, each pattern uses two yarns, mostly held together, but you don't exactly double the yarn needed in comparison to knitting with one yarn, because the stitches formed are worked to a larger gauge together than you would separately. You are using less than you would for two items knitted in a single yarn, but more than

standard stranded colourwork in a balanced chequerboard pattern. The quantity needed of each yarn depends on which is used most to work the single-coloured sections.

How often have you been irritated by having a complete skein or ball of yarn remaining at the end of a project? The extra outlay of cash and the issue of what to do with the leftovers would be nice to avoid, but at the same time oversupply is a whole lot easier than having to track down another one in the same dyelot if the opposite happens and you run out before the project is complete. Frustration both ways, so let's delve into this conundrum a little more.

Having too much yarn left over is the result of a few things. Though it may seem like the quantity of yarn used in a project should be a non-negotiable, fixed thing when worked to the specified gauge in the specified yarn, it still varies from knitter to knitter. This comes from how each of us shape our stitches and, because we are not machines, the variation in our tension (both emotional and strictly gauge-based) throughout a project. To account for all of this, it is standard for designers to specify a little more yarn than the average knitter will use, just to be safe.

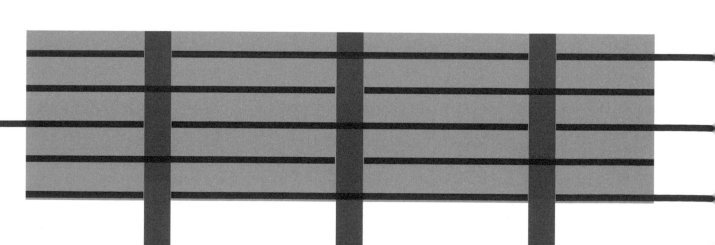

Colour, fibre combination and spin type have roles to play too. The breed of sheep certainly has an effect. In general, woollen-spun yarns will be lighter in weight than worsted-spun ones, so the meterage will be more by weight. The more minimally processed a yarn is, the less it will have been washed, and so will carry more natural lanolin and maybe even vegetable matter to add to its weight. Once yarns are more heavily processed, meterage is known to vary between the paler shades and the darkest, because the weight of the dye starts to play more of role in the overall weight of the yarn.

Then, to exacerbate the situation further, more often than not, yarn companies are generous with how much you actually get in a skein or ball in comparison to what it says on the label. On very odd occasions you may receive one that is under the advertised weight. It's not the done thing to bring scales to your local yarn shop, and when ordering online you are at the whim of what goes into your parcel. Moreover, when a project is offered in multiple sizes, it is impossible (or just not the most interesting design challenge) to make sure that each size uses exactly one extra whole skein or ball than the previous size. So in reality, one of the sizes

will use only a little bit of a skein or ball, whereas others will wrap up perfectly with a quarter of the last skein or ball remaining. None should require you play yarn chicken and finish with just an arm's length to spare. As satisfying and thrilling as that can be if you bring it on yourself, it wouldn't be 'nice' if you were unwittingly forced into that situation by the yarn company or designer, which is why they are both generous with quantities. And when using hand-dyed yarns you have an extra impetus to play it safe and buy enough, or rather, more than enough, to finish your project, because colours may be one-offs or otherwise unrepeatable.

One answer to all of this sometimes appears to be to specify yarn quantity based on total meterage, rather than in terms of skeins and balls — but that is not the route I have taken in this book. Often, when we rely on things being precise, we set ourselves up for disappointment when it still doesn't work out to plan. Too much information can be just as concealing of what you need to know as too little. The yarn quantities specified for each pattern in this book are based on the advertised weight of the specified skein or ball as this is the amount you can get it in from the person who

makes it. If you are trying to use up oddments, you'll generally find some indication in the pattern when smaller garments such as hats and mitts can be worked with half a skein or ball. If you are substituting yarn, the amounts specified should give you enough of a starting point to calculate how much of your chosen yarn you are likely to need, taking into account the many factors at play. The plan is that you will have enough yarn to finish your project and ideally have no more than half a skein or ball left over. And if, despite all our best efforts, you come up short, then ask around — at your local yarn shop, or knit night, or online — and with luck your opposite is out there, wondering what to do with their leftovers. As crafty and creative folks, we can always work out what to do with extra yarn eventually, but we are usually happy to see it used by others in instant need!

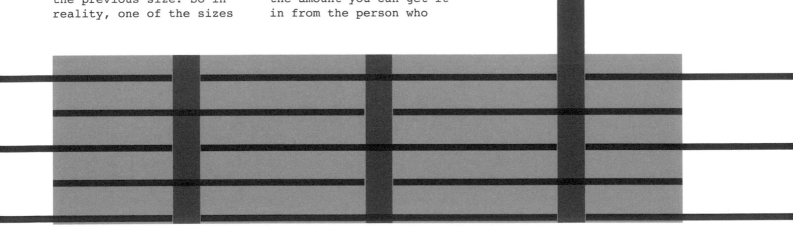

colour and texture.
marlisle has it both.

how to choose your colours.

Finding just the right combo should make your heart sing, your eyes zing and your fingers itch to get started.

You want your two colours to look nice together. It is hard to advise on what 'nice' means, because it depends wholly on your personal taste. Personal taste is influenced by societal norms that vary geographically. Availability, gender and status all play a part alongside other factors. So to start the process of choosing colours, I suggest you trust yourself. Think about what will slot into your existing wardrobe, or the new direction you wish to take.

To get an idea of what the two colours will look like together when marled, try twisting them together as if plying the two yarns into one.

Sticking with a natural undyed and a dyed yarn is a safe bet and the approach used for all the samples in this book. Branching out, it's good to remember that, when it comes to Marlisle, quite unusual combinations can work well. There have been surprises both ways: pleasant ones as the result of combining mint and canary yellow or maroon and bright blue, and a puzzling one where an un-dyed brown and white failed to do justice to them-selves, each other, or the pattern.

Hold both colours up together and squint at them to check they have enough contrast between them.

For Marlisle, the two colours need to be clearly different from each other in order to create a separate third colour when combined. Think of it as blending your own new colour from two existing colours for the marl sections. You will get the clearest results if the colours vary in both shade (think light and dark) and hue (for example red and green, or yellow and grey). This is especially important for Marlisle patterns that include full rounds of standard stranded colourwork, such as the Trembling Sweater (page 130) and Delftig Mittens (page 72). For these, it's generally a good idea to pick two colours that hold their own when worked next to each other. The strong contrast will highlight the work you put in forming the stitches. You'll notice that the two versions of the Trembling Sweater pictured show combinations that are very different in terms of how much 'pop' the shades have together.

Both are worked on a pale, natural grey that leans towards brown. In the combo worn by Adam, where a dark green was used, the pattern is strikingly clear. Worked in the pale minty green (as worn by Marilla) a subtle effect is achieved. While this functions very well in real life, it mutes the details needed in pattern photographs where instructional information needs to be communicated. As long as you are happy to 'lose' some of a pattern's graphic impact, closely related shades can be used successfully. Partly this is down to the fact that I have built textural difference into Marlisle's stitch structures, with areas of stocking stitch framed by reverse stocking stitch or garter stitch.

nothing beats casting on a section!

variegated yarn.

To make it easy for you to see what is going on, all of the dyed yarns in this book are a solid or semi-solid colour. This is not necessary to make a successful garment, but is useful in communicating the construction of the garment clearly in the photographs. When you are choosing your own colour combinations, I recommend that at least one of the yarns should be a solid/semi-solid colour. Nice effects can be achieved by introducing a variegated yarn as one of the colours. Without being able to predict where colours interact, using two variegated yarns or a variegated yarn in combination with a colour that picks up a dominant colour in the variegated yarn risks losing the pattern you are working to build. If using a semi-solid yarn with distinct colour fluc-tuations or a variegated yarn, it's worth reading the notes on colour pooling on page 146.

extra colours.

All of the Marlisle projects in this book are knitted using two colours of yarn at a time. With these two colours you make three (each colour used solo and both in combination). Though it isn't illustrated here, further colours can be introduced in stripes by changing both yarns at once for clearer stripes or maintain one colour consistently and only switch out the other for a subtler effect. This opens up a lot of avenues to explore. It can be a great way to use up single balls or oddments. If you're interested in this angle, the Ess Shawl (page 84) will be a perfect starting point for you (and you'll find a lot of options suggested there).

more than two yarns.

Generally, using two yarns at a time is the way to go. If you use more than two, the difference in weight between the 'marl' and 'isle' sections will be more, perhaps too, significant. You'll also add physical complications when it comes to holding and working with the different yarns. It's not impossible, so let's just call it 'advanced' to the point of being worth dismissing for now.

stitch structure.

The textural possibilities of Marlisle are embedded in the pattern designs by using areas of stocking stitch off-set by garter stitch or reverse stocking stitch. Think of texture as playing almost an equal role to colour.

If you remove the second colour from standard stranded colourwork, to work it in a single colour, you are left with nothing of the pattern-ing. Only the form of the garment remains. The stitch structures of Marlisle can be worked in a single yarn (that equals the weight of the two combined) and you will still be left with a pattern in the stitch structure. This is be-cause Marlisle uses a lot of purl stitches.

With shining exceptions mostly from the Bohus studio, this is unusual in colourwork. By being knitted in the round, most standard stranded colourwork is formed of only knit stitches, with all floats on the back. This way you only need to focus on the colour changes and not between knit and purl. Marlisle has purls on the right side too. But why so many of them?

a whole lotta PURL.

Marlisle patterns using reverse stocking stitch as the 'background' involve a lot of purl stitches. Garter stitch worked in the round requires working alternating rounds of knit and purl. In comparison to reverse stocking stitch, it has the bonus of involv-ing knit rounds (for those who don't like purling). There's a theory on the unknitterly lack of support for purls in the opening story of the Mid-stream Sweater (page 94). You will find both garter stitch and reverse stock-ing stitch used as a foil for the motifs in this book. You'll even find that the Selbbob Hat (page 124) uses a stocking-stitch marl background. Each has distinct benefits in specific patterns. In general, reverse stocking stitch maintains a more similar gauge to stocking stitch. Garter stitch adds more in terms of the squooshiness of the knit. It also adds dynamic move-ment, as the size of the stitches are different to those produced when working only knit stitches in the round.

another practical reason.

When you knit by hand using two yarns of different colours held together, you can't guarantee which one will be dominant on the front of the stitch as you work it. This is possible on a knitting machine, with the addition of a small device called a plater (you can read a snippet more on this in the Yarn Pairing Notes for the Midstream Sweater (page 94)). Marlisle uses textural differences between the knitted 'isle' and the varying 'marl' stitches in order to make the patterns 'pop' where they would otherwise get lost in the inevitable randomness of marl.

yarn texture.

Even more texture can be introduced with the yarns you choose. Especially when you work with less strong contrasts in regards to colour, it can be nice to replace that one form of contrast with another. Textural rich-ness can be introduced, for example, by using a glossy yarn in combina-tion with a matte yarn. This works particularly well in patterns such as the Shantay Cardigan (page 54), Kraai Mitts (page 30) and Midstream Sweater (page 94). You can of course opt for both, as you will find illustrated in the Chevre and Gingham Cowls (pages 118 and 48), which both use a glossy, worsted-spun yarn from a longhaired breed in combination with a plump, matte, woollen-spun yarn. In this way, a small and comparatively quick-to-knit item such as a cowl has all sorts of layers of interest worked in.

other choices.

Knitting is all about making choices. Unlike many choices you have to make in life, the ones that pertain to knitting are satisfyingly contained, achievable and for the most part, reversible.

This is what allows knitting to be relaxing, even when choosing is involved. As the options don't end once the pattern and yarn have been selected, this section will help guide you through the additional decisions you will need to make. They will also offer some insight into how I made my own choices when writing this book.

sizing.

A spread of sizes, measurements and options are offered for each project. There are schematic drawings with clear indications of where measurements are taken from. Photographs and notes give guidance on the intended fit. You can use this information to scale up or down, should you have the knowledge and inclination to get a more personally tailored fit for your garment.

There was a time when having three sizes provided for a sweater was considered a luxury — they showed how to scale up and down from a median with significantly more ease than

simply looking at a picture (or sweater). That approach highlighted the responsibility of the knitter in finding the fit they want, in a way we have become unaccustomed to with ready-to-wear clothing and patterns in correlating sizing. Contemporary patterns have more generous standards. Both the Midstream and Trembling Sweaters (pages 94 and 130) come in six sizes and the Shantay Cardigan (page 54) in five sizes. All the garments for smaller body parts (mittens, mitts, hats and cowls) come in three sizes. The Ess Shawl (page 84) comes in two sizes. The Ruperto Scarf (page 110) comes in a single size, with advice on how to make it longer or shorter.

For modern-day, quick satisfaction, the idea is that you should be able to find dimensions that work for you among those on offer. If that is not the case, some old-fashioned nous can be applied to the information available for you to base your own calculations on. There are many reasons you might want to change things up. Being able to tailor things to your (or the lucky recipient's) particular body quirks and how you like your knits to fit, look and roll off your needles, is part of why we make things ourselves. Where colourwork is involved, however, the process of designing — and

adapting patterns — becomes more complicated. It's not as simple as adding a stitch here and there (which is more easily possible with single-colour knits): there are pattern repeats to consider. Keep an eye on the Pattern Notes and elsewhere in the specific pattern you are working, as they often include tips on how to modify to accommodate for fit and gauge. The Midstream Sweater (page 94) has a particularly nice section on how to adapt it for different body and fit preferences.

naming size.

Size matters, but mostly because of the filters we see it through. Here's an outline of why and how the things that you do need to measure have been approached, all with practical application in mind.

I have called the sizes Extra Small (XS), Small (S), Medium (M), Large (L), Extra Large (XL) and Extra Extra Large (XXL). These are used as comparative terms. They could just have easily been referred to as 1, 2, 3, 4, 5 and 6. However, 1, 2, 3, etc tend to be based on XS, S, M, etc in everything but name, so the source has been stuck with. Beyond being a question of semantics, using these standard size-related letters can help to avoid confusion between numbers that must be used in the pattern (for the likes of stitches and repeats). Similarly, using A, B, C, etc for sizing can create an easy mix-up with Yarn A and B. In general, a quicker connection can be made to garment-sizing using recognisable abbreviations. They are not an invitation to not check the schematic measurements to confirm you are choosing the right size.

Absolutely no value judgement is intended in using these terms, though I do acknowledge they come with some societal baggage. With the tremendous range of body types in the world, there are no universal sizing standards — each system attempts to reflect its local market.

Sizes in this particular collection are based on finding a decent spread within what was possible in the Marlisle stitch structures and in reference to the industry-standard size guides of the Craft Yarn Council of America and those produced by Ysolda Teague. They place a western, Caucasian, 'able' body type central. I have used their sizes intended for adult, non-pregnant women, though those are not the only bodies these knits will look great on. With so much amazing variety between bodies, these are the most useful standards available to work with when making patterns to cater for a generic group. A group that I trust has the smarts to fiddle where they need to, and understands the amazing stretchy power of knitted fabric.

taking measurements.

To measure yourself, get out your tape measure, strip down as far as you feel comfy and grab a friend — together you can reach and read the parts you can't alone. Plus, if you measure them too, it's really insightful to know how much we all vary. Allow a smidgen of breathing space between you and the tape measure. Make sure to note exactly what you are measuring as you write the measurements down.

garment not body measurements.

Measurements shown on the pattern schematic always relate to the garment, not to the related body part. For example, you can expect the sleeves to be shorter than your arms, and wider at the top than your actual top-of-arm measurements. This is so your cuffs don't hang over your hands and you can get in and out of your sweater or cardigan. Similarly, a cowl needs to fit over your head, in order to fit round your skinnier neck.

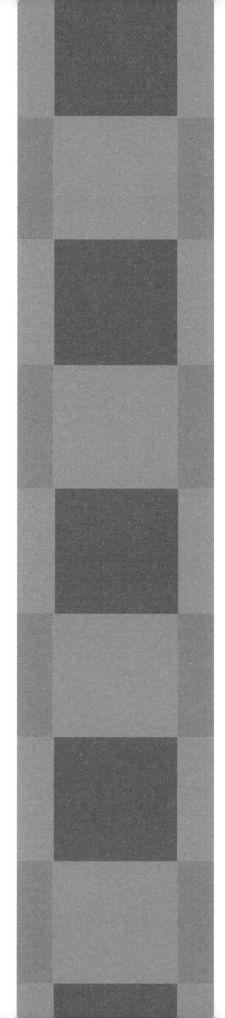

needles.

Each pattern clearly outlines suggested needle size. This is for guidance only, which is why you will find the mantra 'Always use a needle size that will result in the correct gauge after blocking' in each project. Consider the needle sizes and type on offer as the starting point for your search for the one that will work for you to achieve the specified gauge with your chosen yarn and the way you knit.

size.

If you want to try a different approach to working out what needle size to use for Marlisling, start your experiments on the lightest yarn you will be working a stocking-stitch motif in and add 1mm to the needle size you would usually use for that weight of yarn. This way, if you use a 3mm for 4ply/fingering yarn, add 1mm needle size, so you start your experimenting with a 4mm needle. If you generally use a 4.5mm for DK/light worsted yarn, give 5.5mm a go to start with. US needle sizes work a little differently, but in general, go up two sizes from what you would usually reach for for a specific yarn weight. If designing your own project, or substituting the yarn for one with a very different character, it also totally depends on what you want your fabric to be like — holey-ness can be part of the plan for some projects,

whereas if you are making mittens, you want something nice and dense to help protect your hands from the elements.

type.

All of the projects in this book are worked primarily in the round (the exceptions are a few instances of set-up rows and short rows). This means they are designed to be worked on circular needles (with or without a magic loop) and DPNs, not good old straight needles. You'll notice that some patterns specify simply 'needles suitable for working small circumferences in the round' for areas of the pattern, such as cuffs, or whole accessories, such as mittens, that are a narrow tube. In those cases you'll want to use your favourite approach to working a small number of stitches in the round and the corresponding needle type that works best for you.

points.

In general, the type of needle tip is down to your personal preference. However, when working the bobbles for the Selbbob Hat (page 124) you will benefit from using needles with pointy tips (often called lace needles), as explained in the pattern instructions. You may find elsewhere that blunter tips work better with the multiple yarns of Marlisle, as they are less likely to further split one of the single strands.

There's good reason for the mantra :
'Always use a needle size
that will result in the
correct gauge after blocking'

cast-ons and cast-offs.

Guidance is given for the type of cast-on or cast-off to use for each project, often with a pointer as to how or why that specific one is used, with, at times, possible alternatives. If it is an unfamiliar cast-on to you, it's worth pausing to learn (from whatever kind of tutorial works best for you) and use it as it will benefit the project. The same goes for cast-offs. In both cases, if you have a wide range of choices in your arsenal, by all means, use your own good judgement. The long-tail cast-on makes regular appearances, as it is a good all-purpose method if you will be working in the round directly after you cast on (and need a moderate amount of stretch).

A word of warning:
In Marlisle patterns, a tendency to cast on too tightly can be exacerbated by the fact that generally, Marlisle cast-ons are worked with a single yarn, rather than both held together, so take particular care. They are worked in a single colour because, practicality-wise, it's easier to count how many stitches you have when using a single yarn, but also as an aesthetic choice of how to start/finish the projects off. When casting off in Marlisle, however, there is more leeway — for

both aesthetics AND technical reasons — and you can work the cast-off with either of the two yarns singly, both together or a combination thereof. It is important to ensure that your cast-on or cast-off has sufficient stretch to work with the project. In general, if you are inclined to tight cast-ons and cast-offs, using a larger needle size when it comes time to work them can be a quick fix.

When working a long-tail cast-on, be aware that the tightness may come from the yarn over your thumb (forming the base-loops), rather than from the one wrapping around the needle.

If you are substituting yarns,
it is worth giving some consideration to which yarn you use to cast on or cast off with, for a few reasons. Avoid using the most delicate or likely to pill of your two yarns. Consider which colour will show dirt least, as edges always get grubbiest. When choosing between yarns that vary in texture, use the smoothest. If you are using two different weight yarns for the project, always choose the thicker of the two, so that it takes up the most space and will correspond to the gauge of the project. You need the cast-on to be

big, bulky and stretchy enough to be worked into during the next round, where many of the stitches will be worked with both yarns held together, making for fatter stitches. And you don't want the cast-off to gather up what you have done before or hamper the natural stretch of the knitted fabric.

A single-yarn edge might be be slightly less hard-wearing than a doubled-up one, but you wouldn't even begin to notice this unless you wear your garment EVERY SINGLE DAY straight for many YEARS. Which of course I hope you do.

A cast-off tip for when working in the round:
Start your cast-off with a knit-front-and-back (kfb), then cast those 2 stitches off on themselves and continue casting off until 2 stitches remain, knit 2 stitches together (k2tog), then cast off the 2 remaining stitches on your needle. This helps prevent the unsatisfying join you ordinarily get between the little dip as you start your cast off and the slight peak when you finish. This will come in particularly useful in the Midstream Sweater (page 94) and Kraai Mitts (page 30) as they both have a cast-off that starts in a visible spot.

the fabric.

Whether tight or loose, the density of a knitted fabric is an intrinsic part of what makes a successful garment.

Because Marlisle comprises some areas of two yarns held together and others where they are worked singly, you are looking for a density of fabric that works in both. To achieve this, you are aiming for a comparatively more compact fabric in the 'marl' section, and a more open motif 'isle' section. 'Isle' sections will be a different density to the marled sections, but the overall fabric will be of a fairly equivalent thickness, owing to the floats behind the 'isle'. In a sense, you are aiming for your 'marl' sections to be a little tighter than usual (without being stiff as a board) and your 'isle' sections to be a little looser (without being holey). These are not hard-and-fast rules, as they can be a fun jumping-off point for further textural experimentation. But they are useful to adhere to as you start. If this seems unusual, keep in mind that similar fluctuations in knit density happen when you work cables, or a sweater with a stranded colourwork yoke on a plain stocking stitch body.

What complicates things is that there really isn't a useful 'usual'. Socks require a very different 'usual' to a lace shawl and a Cornish knit frock has quite a different 'usual' to a lopapeysa. They each have their place and are a reflection of the style, application and history of the garment. It's comforting to note that densely knitted projects tend to rate well in terms of longevity in comparison to loose knits. In cold-weather climates, being able to put another layer on and wrap up warm has benefits in terms of energy consumption.

Though all the patterns specify a gauge to aim for, this is based on what will get you a garment of the same proportions. The gauge only helps you know what density of fabric is being called for if you use the specified yarns. It remains only part of the story of how to achieve either the fabric I intended when I designed it or the one you feel works for the garment you are after.

gauge and/or tension.

While deliberating whether to go with the more North America-centric 'gauge' or British 'tension' in this book, a wise woman (trained in psychology), made the point that tension of any sort was best avoided. Though there are places tension can be useful, best not to avoid or pleasurable, when it comes to knitting I think she had a good point. You will find 'gauge' used for the description of how many stitches and how many rounds (not rows) you should be looking for to have the pattern instructions work, which frees up 'tension' to be used more descriptively in relation to how you hold your yarn and for things such as floats.

measuring gauge.

All gauges specified in this book are given for measurements after blocking. This means that you should soak and block your swatch, as you would your finished knit, before measuring your stitch and round counts. Washing is especially important when using undyed yarns, as they often have been far less processed than dyed yarns, so are likely to bloom much more than a yarn that has been heated in a dye kettle and rinsed repeatedly. This means there will be a more significant change before and after a soak. Because of the interplay of sections of two yarns held together and single-yarn motif sections, it becomes more

complicated to work out the average gauge across
the whole fabric. The average gauge will depend
on the regularity of the use of both types of
stitches. This is not dissimilar to cable
knitting, however, where the overall fabric will
vary based on whether the cabling is dense on
the whole body or whether there is just a single
cable running up the centre. The best approach
to measuring is to have as large a section as
possible to take the 10cm/4″ measurements from,
so you can check in different places to see if
they are the same. Make sure you are not measuring at the very edge of a project or swatch, as
the edge will distort the measurements you take.
This is why it is suggested you make a swatch
that is bigger than 10cm x 10cm/4″ x 4″, so that
you can measure in the centre of it.

swatching.

Just do it (or be comfortable embracing the consequences). That's good general advice, but, where Marlisle is concerned, there's additional reason to observe it. In that it is an unusual approach to knitting, it is unlikely you have worked in this way before, so it is harder to rely on the knowledge you have built up in other projects in the way an inveterate sock knitter or 4ply/fingering-weight sweater knitter might. Your gauge relies on two yarns frequently worked together that are often different from each other.

There are those who don't swatch because they are so keen to get started. Others trust as gospel the gauge and needle-size relation-ship (given as helpful guidance) as if it were written just for them rather than the mythical Average Knitter. Another category of knitter subscribes to the idea that there's no point, because the garment will come out different from expected regardless of whether you swatch or not. Then there's the camp who secretly enjoy swatching more than making the finished item. This reminder to swatch is not for them. It's the middle two groups whom I'd like to impress upon a little by talking through how to work a swatch that will hopefully give more accurate results, not just in unfamiliar Marlisle territory, but for whenever swatching would next be appropriate.

If there is a particular approach to swatching that suits specific projects, guidance is given in the pattern as a 'Swatching Note' under 'Gauge'. Basically, it is best to replicate what you will do to make the garment as closely as possible while you are swatching. This also encourages you to practise and go over the specifics of the pattern a little beforehand. It goes without saying that you should use the same yarns, ideally down to the same dyelot or batch. There can be significant fluctuations from year to year or from batch to batch, particularly in small-run yarns or if mills and machinery have been changed. You'll find a lengthy description of how to work a circular swatch with a knotted steek outlined later on, another one in Felicity Ford's *Knitsonik Stranded Colourwork Sourcebook*, if you have it on your bookshelf. A good online tutorial for the knotted steek can be found from Tom van Deijnen at www.tomofholland.com/2014/04/20/knit-and-knot-knotted-steek-tutorial.

All of the projects in this book are worked in the round, so your swatches should be worked in the round too for increased accuracy and consistency of gauge. Working a flat swatch for a round project is the first place you are likely to create discrepancies. Lots of knitters find they get a different gauge depending on if they are knitting flat as opposed to in the round, whether they are working knit, purl or some combination thereof, and even what type of needles they are using (wood, metal, straight, round, DPN, magic looping). Personally, my gauge is the same whether I am knitting in the round on circulars that are the right length to easily accommodate all the stitches or on DPNS, but it varies if I use the magic-loop method. Be sure you are paying attention to row gauge as well as to stitch gauge, especially in projects such as hats and sweaters. Don't be annoyed if your gauge does vary for any of these reasons, just be aware and account for it.

When working a gauge swatch, use the same cast-on and cast-off method specified for the project. You can read more about cast-ons and cast-offs on page 19. Make sure to cast on 1.5 times the number of stitches the gauge specifies for 10cm/4". Where multiple gauges are given, there will be a note to say which is most important. If you are aiming to get 24 stitches per 10cm/4", then cast on 24 stitches, plus 12 (half of 24), for a total of 36 stitches in your pattern zone. You are casting on more stitches than you need for 10cm/4" so that you can take measurements in the centre of your swatch, which should itself be about 15cm/6cm square. Stitches at the edges of a swatch tend to warp and tend not to give an accurate read.

All of the specified gauges are based on the finished projects after they were soaked and blocked, so for the patterns in this book, it is important to do the same to your swatch. Undyed yarns tend to bloom more significantly, because they have not gone through as much processing, so the difference before and after a soak and block will be more noticeable. Soaking will also allow you to see if the yarns you are using are colourfast before you commit to making the garment. You can accommodate accordingly by shortening the soak, using cold water, adding a splash of vinegar or changing the colour combo, so you know what to do when you come to the actual project. As you block your swatch to let it dry, you should not force it to do anything it doesn't want to — don't make it conform to a set of measurements (such as 10cm/4" or 15cm/6") or the gauge you are hoping for. Gently open up the pattern and even out the fabric to see if you can get it to dry into a fabric you like the behaviour of that will work with the pattern requirements.

Read more suggestions about this process in the General Finishing Instructions on page 142.

This particular approach is suggested, because it uses the steek used in three patterns: the Ruperto Scarf (page 110), Ess Shawl (page 84) and Shantay Cardigan (page 54). It will use a lot more yarn than a standard swatch, but you can always undo it (rather than cutting it), if the yarn is needed to finish your project. However, it can be fun and useful to keep your swatches for later reference.

how many stitches to cast on.

Decide how many stitches you need for your swatch pattern zone, based on 1.5 times the number of stitches you need to get 10cm/4", as suggested on page 22. Cast on using the method suggested in the pattern you are swatching for. If it is one that doesn't tell you to join in the round instantly, then work a row(s) as specified.

Then, using the backwards-loop method (what machine knitters call the e-wrap method, because the shape is like writing the letter e repeatedly in cursive), cast on an additional 13 steek stitches. These 13 stitches are cast on using this method because it is easy to undo when you have cut the steek, however, it is a bit of a beast to knit into in the first round, especially when transferring stitches for magic looping. For that reason, make sure you form these loops loosely. Join in the round, being careful not to twist. If for example, 36 stitches represented 1.5 times your gauge needed for 10cm/4", you now have a total of 49 stitches.

the swatch.

The stitch at each edge of the pattern zone (the 36 stitches) will be the Steek Edge Stitches (1 stitch on each side), which frame the pattern zone and create a guideline to make knots along and eventually pick up and knit. Always knit, don't purl, the Steek Edge Stitches in the same single colour throughout. But if you add additional colours, or a motif of the same colour butts up against it, switch to using the contrasting colour, if yarn weight allows. The pattern zone starts at the second stitch of the long-tail cast-on and continues until a single stitch of that cast-on remains. This is the part you work in different combinations of both yarns. The final stitch of the long-tail cast-on section is the other Steek Edge Stitch. This should be worked the same as the first Steek Edge Stitch. Always knit the 13 steek stitches as stocking stitch using both yarns held double, except for the central stitch, number 7, of the steek,

which you should work in the most dominant colour only to make an easy guideline to cut down. You can even use 2 or 3 Steek Edge Stitches on each side, if you want. These are how Decorative Seams (DS) work, which you will find in various Marlisle patterns and are explained in more length in Terminology (page 148).

to cast off.

Using the cast-off method specified in the pattern you are swatching for, cast off the pattern section between and including the first and last Steek Edge Stitches. Do not cast off the steek section, as you will be undoing this anyway.

If there's a chance you may need the yarn, then cast off the lot, leaving a tail that makes it easy to undo if needed. Omit cutting and knotting the steek and jump straight to blocking, adapting the instructions for an uncut steek.

cutting the steek.

When you are satisfied that you're good to go, use a small sharp pair of scissors to cut down the centre of the single-colour guideline stitches in the centre of the steek section from top to cast-on edge to leave 6.5 stitches on either side.

unravelling and knotting the steek.

One round at a time, starting from the top, unravel the 6.5 stitches up to the Steek Edge Stitch. Do not unravel the Steek Edge Stitch. Knot Yarn A&B together using an overhand knot, fastening the knot as close to the Steek Edge Stitch as you can without distorting it. By using the Steek Edge Stitch as a guide, all the knots will be nice and consistently placed. Unravel and then tie each round as you work your way down to the bottom edge, rather than undoing all the rounds at once and risking the confusion of which strands to knot together afterwards. Leave the strands long. Do not trim them yet! You'll learn what to do next on the following page.

●●●

●●●

blocking.

When all the knots are tied, it's time for a
good soak in your favorite wool-friendly detergent.
Leave it to soak for a good half an hour or
more to allow the kinks in the fringing to relax
and the stitches to ease into place. Rinse and
squeeze out water. Do not wring. Wrap in a towel
and stand or sit on it to squeeze out excess
moisture. (If you sit on it, you can play the
silly game of having to guess when to stand up
to avoid a damp bum.)

Encourage your swatch to lie flat after soaking
and pin it out gently. Unlike with a garment,
you are not trying to coax it to adhere to a set
of measurements, but you are trying to train it
to behave like the garment will. Use your
fingers to 'comb' out the fringing. Because these
patterns are not significantly ribbed (when you
don't want to stretch the stitches) or lacey
(which generally means you do want to stretch
the stitches, really hard), you are looking for
something in the middle for your swatch. You are
aiming to open up the pattern and even out the
fabric. You are not blocking it to make it adhere
to the 15cm/6" you are aiming for.

once dry.

You should ideally let your swatch sit for at
least a day before measuring your gauge from it,
so that the stitches have had a chance to
relax. Once dry, comb out the fringing again,
to straighten it. Cut the fringing, leaving
1cm/¼". It's easiest to do this it with a pair
of long, sharp, fabric scissors. You can use
the fringing to make mini pompoms, by gathering
them into a bunch and tying a tight knot
in the centre using cotton or linen in a
sympathetic colour.

working marlisle.

All the elements of Marlisle will be familiar to the average knitter — it's just that the stitches and techniques are configured a little differently.

This next chapter will help you approach the unusual configurations with more confidence. It offers guidance on tailoring how you already knit, so that Marlisle can slot in more intuitively. It also explains some of the reasons why 'odd' choices, such as long floats and lots of purling, are used.

holding yarn.

What characterises Marlisle is that some sections of each pattern are worked using both yarns held together. This is the marl part of Marlisle. When working rounds that are fully marled, you'll hold Yarn A&B together in one hand, treating them as if they were a single yarn. In rounds where both yarns are used, but only ever singly, use your prefered method of holding yarn for standard stranded colour-work; that is exactlly what this is, with the other yarn being a float at the back. This is the fairisle part of Marlisle, which lends the 'isle'. In rounds that involve both 'marl' and 'isle', where either Yarn A and/or B are worked singly and there are sections of A&B worked together, you will need to play around and see what works best for you. Start experimenting, based on how you hold your yarn for standard stranded colourwork — use what is familiar.

There are a million and one ways to hold yarn. Stated simplistically, some knitters hold it in the left hand and some hold it in the right. When doing standard stranded colour-work, some hold one colour in each hand (two-handed colourwork), where others hold both colours in one hand. To tension the yarn, some wrap the yarn multiple times around a single finger or a combination of multiple fingers, where others drape or weave it loosely across their fingers. Some knitters tension their yarn by letting it run round the back of their neck. You may have worked out a system that works for you through trial and error, or many hours of observing other knitters, or by trawling through blogs and tutorials. Especially when it comes to stranded colourwork, knitters get a bee in their bonnet about finding a better way. Often, when something becomes familiar and works for us, it is easy to forget it is A Right Way, rather than The Right Way. Many of us base the Right Way on what we were taught when we learned how to knit. It is what worked for the accomplished knitter who showed us the ropes. It may have been the dominant style in the area in which you learned, or not — knitters travel far and wide, bring-ing with them their skills and sharing them as they go.

Whether you can do it with your eyes closed, or if stranded colourwork of any description is new to you, and/or you are still on the quest to find your way, it would be impossible to say which will be the right way for you. So with apologies, this book will not tell you the hard and fast way to approach this, because there isn't a single way. It depends too much on your existing knowledge and comfort base. Any firm rule that would be given would be based on my personal preferences and experience. To make it even more complicated to find The Rule, when working Marlisle, your project will likely benefit from you using different approaches in different sections of a single pattern. What will work best will vary given the structure and balance of the stitches in different places in the pattern.

Just remember, there's nothing wrong with just dropping the colour you aren't using and picking it up again when you need it. In the sections with floats, you will need to pay attention to your floats having the same tension, but more about that in the dedicated Floats section below. If you can find a comfortable way to hold both yarns, rather than letting go of one, it is likely that you will get more even results and speed up your process (if that is what you are after). Whichever method you use, keep an eye on your float tension, and keeping it consistent enough. Do play around with different ways to hold the yarn more effectively and keep on doing so throughout the pattern.

colour dominance.

Colour dominance is worth giving special consideration to in patterns such as the Delftig Mittens (page 72) and Trembling Sweater (page 130) that involve sections of standard stranded colourwork. Make sure to hold the different yarns in the same place consistently for best results, whether this is the hand you hold each yarn

in or where you place it on your finger — decide and stick with it (write yourself a reminder note!). If that section of pattern involves purling, decide which yarn goes where, based on which holding position works best for you during the purl stitches. In other patterns, the reverse stocking stitch or garter stitch sections of Yarn A&B together create a natural break between the single colours that should even things out without you needing to pay as much attention to colour dominance. Besides, when switching between using one or two colours at a time AND between knit and purl, it's near-impossible to find a consistent way to hold the yarn, but this shouldn't prevent you from developing a comforting rhythm.

floats.

Floats are the lengths of yarn in the colour not in use that span the space between where it was last used to form a stitch and the next place it will be used. When you are marling with both colours held together, there will be no float. In the sections that are not marled, you will have floats. For example, when working with Yarn A only, Yarn B will create a float at the back and vice versa. As with other forms of colourwork that involve stranding, floats longer than 7 stitches are to be avoided, or caught at the back to avoid the risk of snagging. In creating these Marlisle designs, I have mostly steered clear of including floats longer than this, a decision that played into the overall look of the patterns. The sections with floats are generally kept to less than 7 stitches, and the distances between motifs can be

worked using both yarns held together as marl.

Catching floats, aka weaving in the second colour on the wrong side of the work, is usually advised. However this is not the case with Marlisle where the single-colour 'isle' sections rely on being distinct from the marled sections. Catching floats could muddle the effect and therefore I don't recommend it. You will find notes in a couple of patterns where it is necessary to catch floats, but elsewhere, you should try not to. You may have been trained to catch as regularly as every 3 stitches. If you can't shake this 'rule', be sure to vary where you catch your floats to avoid them showing through on the right side (unless you wish to work that into your design). One of the reasons for catching floats is that it helps create an even tension across the fabric, so when not catching floats, pay extra attention to the tension of your floats so that their stretchiness, or lack thereof, does not unduly affect the fabric.

Some knitters who find it hard to regulate the tension of their floats (or who simply like having a clear view of them as they work) choose to work inside out, with the floats facing them. This can be particularly helpful when working corrugated rib in order to prevent it getting too tight. This is something you may wish to consider if you are making the Selbbob Hat (page 124).

Usually, floats are kept on the wrong side of the work, but on some of the intentionally reversible fabrics in this book, such as the Ess Shawl (page 84) and Ruperto Scarf (page 110), they can become a feature. As a designer, I feel like it is my responsibility make both sides of the fabric satisfying to look at if they will both be visible, or if you might want it to be reversible for another reason. Floats can become a deliberate part of the design, rather than just an unavoidable consequence. This is particularly pertinent when it comes to scarves, shawls, blankets and cowls. With these, you will want to make extra sure that your floats are a similar gauge throughout (although a lot will even out in the soaking and blocking process). If you want to get more elaborate, you can double-knit the single-colour sections, separating the two yarns used together in the previous round to start using them separately, one for each side. This would work especially well in a pattern such as the Gingnam Cowl (page 48).

the patterns.

KRAAI

/krʌɪ/

In Dutch, *kraai* means crow. In English, when we speak of distances travelled in a straight line, regardless of the path of roads and natural or constructed boundaries that would otherwise further add to them — legal obstacles such as borders or those that would be insurmountable by foot, such as oceans, rivers, deserts, mountains and ravines — we say that this is 'as the crow flies'. In Dutch this is *vogelvlucht* or *hemelsbreed*, referencingbirds' flight in general, or the width of the heavens.

Travelling home, in wonderful company, from the Edinburgh Yarn Festival a couple of years ago, I was marvelling at the fact that we must be on the slowest train ever, because we could have travelled from King's Cross to Paris in half the time it was taking to get back to London. Because the UK doesn't 'do' high-speed trains like the TGV or Shinkansen, I was making assumptions, laying blame at the tracks of the plodding train system. Adam decided to do a little instant on-line research and we discovered that it wasn't the train's (lack of) speed that made for the long journey, but the actual miles being covered — we were travelling nearly double the distance. Perhaps influenced by having spent a weekend around yarns mostly from the UK and proudly so, this surprised me. I've stood on the beach at Dover on a clear day and seen Calais, but some-how Scotland seemed closer, because no passport is required (currently). Coming from the UK, a smallish country, I usually thought of 'Made in the UK' as a way to judge what is local, not as a label of nationalism.

Realising just how far away Scotland was, I started considering the peripheral islands of the UK. As wool is never far from my mind, I thought especially of places strongly associated with knitting and distinct breeds of sheep: Shetland and the Outer Hebrides. A few months before, I had flown to Shetland from Edinburgh. Flying there by plane had taken an hour; what felt like 10 minutes of which over mainland Scotland, and the rest over the ocean until crests of waves became visible as the plane descended and we landed at Sumburgh airport. Combining these two journeys — one by train and one by plane — I calculated the *vogelsflucht* mileage involved and where else that could get me if I were to look outside the national borders of the UK.

yarn pairing notes.

As the crow flies, then, the yarns used in the Kraai mitts are distinctly bound to places that are practically equidistant to my base in London. Travelling 513 miles northwest will get me to the tiny Isle of Berneray in the Outer Hebrides. Here, Meg Rodger raises the sheep that produce the fleece for her Birlinn Yarn Company yarns, which are a mix of Hebridean and Cheviot that gives a satisfying depth of colour when dyed. Meg's flock are more used to sailing than flying, as that is their main form of transit between islands.

Travelling 545 miles from my home in Hackney, in the opposite direction, will get me to the Filature du Valgaudemar mill in St Firmin, southeastern France. The mill, founded by Geraldine Allemand's grandfather, spins many different yarns, using a range of fibres of diverse origin. I have used her Valgaudemar 2 Fils, which uses the same yarn structure that was originally spun from the fleece of sheep that were grazed around the mill in her grandfather's day. There are no sheep there now, but today's fleeces still come from within France. All seven available shades are undyed: four are solids and three are marled.

construction and fit.

A speedy, engrossing little project inspired by old fashioned leather driving gloves with arrows on the fronts that echo birds in flight or road markings. The short Cuff is ribbed on the palm side only, framing the front and back of the mitts. Your round starts in the centre of this ribbing. The central of these five single-colour ribs splits in two to make six single-colour ribs. These six ribs extend up and out using travelling stitches to meet on the front side of the mitt as the three points of the decorative arrow motif. The first 3 single-colour stitches knitted at the start of each round are a Decorative Seam (DS) that appears in many of the other Marlisle patterns. It obscures the jog that would otherwise occur when garter stitch is worked in the round (which requires alternating one round of knit, then purl, rather than consistently knitting every row as you do to for garter stitch when working flat). The start of the round always hugs the edge of the first 3-st rib (where the rib splits) throughout the mitt. Though the total number of stitches remains consistent in the Hand, the start of the round shifts over to the left with the decrease that happens at the start of every other round in the Hand. The decrease is replaced by an increase at the end of the same round. For the most part, every decrease is balanced out and replaced by an increase, making a fabric that runs on a sort of double-bias, which is why the chart runs with a slant to the left. The only unbalanced increases happen at the end of the Cuff, to go into the Hand to make for a well-fitting mitt with a narrower Cuff than Hand. There are also unbalanced decreases in the final rounds, to stop the mitts from flaring out with wear and movement.

Buttonhole construction is used for the thumb-hole, the only part of the mitt that is worked differently to accommodate for right and left hand.

sizing.

S (M, L)
Designed to be worn with minimal ease around hand.

yarn.

Yarn A: Filature Valgaudemar, Valgaudemar 2 Fils (4ply/fingering; 100% French wool; 175m/191yds per 50g/1¾oz)
Burel x 1

Yarn B: Birlinn Yarn Company, 4ply (4ply/fingering; 100% wool, Hebridean and Cheviot blend; 175m/191yds per 50g/1¾oz)
Reef or Moor x 1

You will likely be able to knit a pair of size S mitts using just half a skein of Yarn A, but you will need more than half for both size M and L. Because most of the patterning happens in Yarn B, count on needing a full ball of that.

worn by...

Anna in Burel and Moor, size S, knitted by Anna Maltz.
Just visible is the Hozkwoz Hat (page 40) and a pink and orange dress sewn (and dyed) by Marilla Walker from her Isca pattern.
Adam in Burel and Reef, size L, knitted by Anna Maltz.

gauge.

22 stitches x 40 rows = 10cm x 10cm/4" x 4" over garter stitch using Yarn A&B held together after blocking.

You are after a dense fabric in the Yarn A&B garter-stitch sections, so that the Yarn B-only decorative arrows aren't holey.

Note: You can chose to knit a circular swatch (see note in The Fabric chapter, page 23) or simply start knitting a mitt, because it is almost the same size as the swatch you would work anyway. If you get gauge, continue with your mitt. If not, this was not a mitt, it was just a swatch. If it is a swatch, don't undo it until you can compare it with the other(s) to see which you prefer.

needles.

3.25mm (US3) needles suitable for working small circumferences in the round.

Always use a needle size that will result in the correct gauge after blocking.

notions.

tapestry needle
stitch marker

glossary.

splitA&B
Using Yarn A&B held together, knit into the Yarn A and Yarn B sections of next stitch individually, as if they were 2 separate stitches. 1-st increase.

LLI
Left-leaning lifted increase. Work a stitch into the left shoulder of the stitch in the row below the stitch you have just worked. 1-stitch increase.

RLI
Right-leaning lifted increase. Work a stitch into the right shoulder of the stitch in the row below the next stitch. 1-stitch increase.

pattern notes.

BOR: If using magic loop or DPNs, it's a good idea to shift where on your needles your BOR is at regular intervals for a couple of reasons. It will help you circumvent any habits you have of pulling too tight or loose at the start of a new round and prevent lines from forming at transitions between needles. It will make sense as you work decs and make it easier to work the decs themselves.

Decrease method substitute: You can replace the ssk with an k2tog tbl throughout the pattern when working the travelling sts. The ssk suggested is a little slower to work than a k2tog tbl, but will result in a smoother line.

---

schematic.

hand circumference
20 (22, 23.5)cm
8 (8½, 9¼)"

length
15 (16, 17)cm
6 (6½, 6¾)"

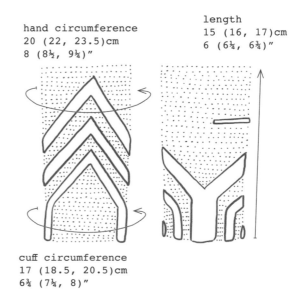

cuff circumference
17 (18.5, 20.5)cm
6¾ (7¼, 8)"

pattern begins.

Using Yarn B and the long-tail method, loosely cast on 39 (43, 47) sts. Join in the round being careful not to twist. PM to mark BOR.

cuff.

Work from Cuff chart or written instructions for your size.
Round 1 (Row 1 of Cuff chart): K2B, [p2 (2, 3)A&B, k3B] twice, p15 (19, 19)A&B, [k3B, p2 (2, 3)A&B] twice, k2B.
Round 2 (Row 2 of Cuff chart): K2B, [k2 (2, 3)A&B, k3B] twice, k15 (19, 19)A&B, [k3B, k2 (2, 3)A&B] twice, k2B.

Repeat Rounds 1-2 a total of 5 times. Cuff should measure 2.5cm/1" from cast-on.

Next round (Row 3 of Cuff chart): Repeat Round 1 once more.

Note: You will want to catch your Yarn A floats a couple of times over the 8 Yarn B stitches that span the beginning and end of chart Row 4 of Cuff and Rows 1-2 of the Hand.

Next round (Row 4 of Cuff chart) (inc): K1B, M1LB, k1B, [k1 (1, 2)A&B, splitA&B, k3B] twice, k15 (19, 19)A&B, [k3B, k1 (1, 2)A&B, splitA&B] twice, k1B, M1RB, k1B.
(6 sts inc) *45 (49, 53) sts*

hand.

Work from Hand chart for your size. You should have 45 (49, 53) sts at the end of each round, until you cast off for the Thumbhole. Below are Rounds 1-2 written out, to get you started.

Round 1 (Row 1 of Hand chart): K3B, [p3 (3, 4)A&B, k3B] twice, p15 (19, 19)A&B, [k3B, p3 (3, 4)A&B] twice, k3B.
Round 2 (Row 2 of Hand chart): K2B, sskB, [k1 (1, 2) A&B, splitA&B, k2B, sskB] twice, k13 (17, 17)A&B, [k2tog, k2B, splitA&B, k1 (1, 2)A&B] twice, k2tog, k2B, LLI A&B, RLI A&B.

thumbhole.

Thumbholes are placed differently for right and left mitt as shown on chart. Only work one Thumbhole per mitt. Work cast-off and cast-on using Yarn A&B.

Round 25 (27, 29) (Thumbhole cast-off round):
Work Row 25 (27, 29) of chart to where indicated for right OR left Thumbhole depending on which hand you are working, purl to loosely cast off 10 (10, 11) sts, finish round according to chart. *35 (39, 42) sts*

Round 26 (28, 30) (Thumbhole cast-on round): Work Row 26 (28, 30) of chart to the start of where you cast off sts in the previous round. To cast on, turn your work so the sts you have just worked are on the left needle, rather than the right.

To cast on the first st, lift a leg from the first cast-off st from row below, twist it anti-clockwise and place on left needle. This becomes the first st of the 10 (10, 11) sts needed to replace those sts cast off in the round below. Now insert the needle between this new st and last st knitted to work a cable cast-on. Make a new st and put it on the left needle. Continue with the cable cast-on until you have a total of 9 (9, 10) new sts. Start making the 10th (10th, 11th) st, but before putting the new loop on to the left needle, move the yarns forward (from back to front) between the sts (the last one knitted and the one you are just finishing), then put the new st on left needle. This puts the yarns on the correct side so you can turn the work and start knitting. Work to end of round according to chart. For the Left Hand only, work the highlighted inc (directly after the cast-on) as a kfb, rather than a splitA&B inc, for strength. *45 (49, 53) sts*

both hands again.

Continue working from Row 27 (29, 31) of chart, maintaining a constant st count of 45 (49, 53) sts up to and including Row 39 (43, 47).

decreases.

The decreases at the top of the mitt stop the edge from flaring out around the fingers. They are worked according to the chart with the same sk2po dec you have been using to taper the tips of the previous two arrows, but unlike previously, the decs are NOT replaced by the usual splitA&B incs to either side.

Round 40 (44, 48) (dec): (2 sts dec) *43 (47, 51) sts*
Round 42 (46, 50) (dec): (2 sts dec) *41 (45, 49) sts*
Round 44 (48, 52) (dec): (2 sts dec) *39 (43, 47) sts*

Work 3 more rounds to end of chart. You have now finished working from the chart.

Cast off loosely using Yarn A&B. See the cast-off tip on page 19 for the inside scoop on smooth results when starting and finishing your cast-off in such a visible place.

Make the second mitt in the same way, remembering that the Thumbhole will be placed differently on other Hand as given in chart and written instructions (otherwise, on one Hand, you will have the arrows on your palm).

special finishing instructions.

Take a little extra care when weaving in the ends from the cast-off as they fall in the centre of the front of the mitts. Soak, squeeze out excess water and block to size, giving a good tug to help tame the travelling-stitches section. Allow to dry flat, folded in half so that the arrows fall in the centre of the front of the mitt and the Thumbholes are on the right or left side of the edge of the back, depending on Hand.

size S.

hand.

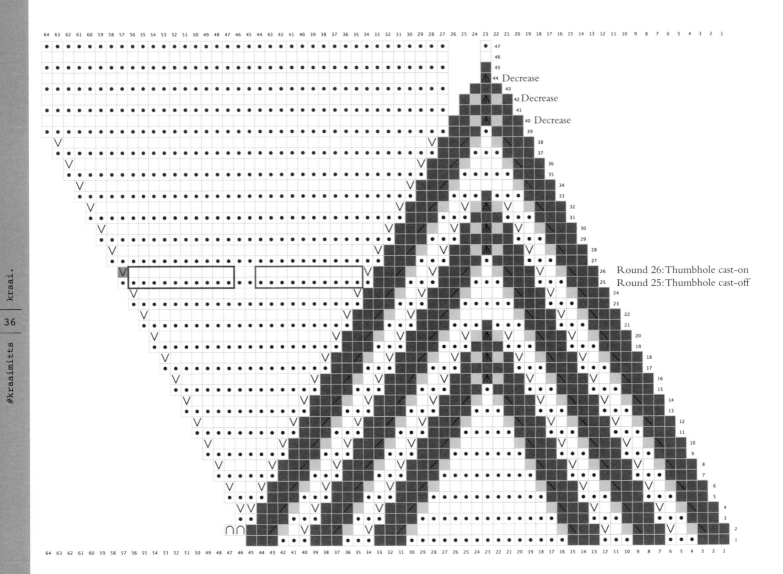

Round 26: Thumbhole cast-on
Round 25: Thumbhole cast-off

44 Decrease
42 Decrease
40 Decrease

cuff.

key.

■	Worked with Yarn B only, with Yarn A held at back
□	Worked with Yarn A&B held together
□	knit
•	purl
□	Cuff repeat
Y	M1L

V	splitA&B
Y	M1R
\	ssk
▨	no stitch
/	k2tog

∩	lifted increase, work first one as left-leaning and second as right-leaning
□	Right Thumbhole
□	Left Thumbhole
∧	sk2po
▨	Work as kfb with Yarn A&B on left mitt ONLY

size M.

hand.

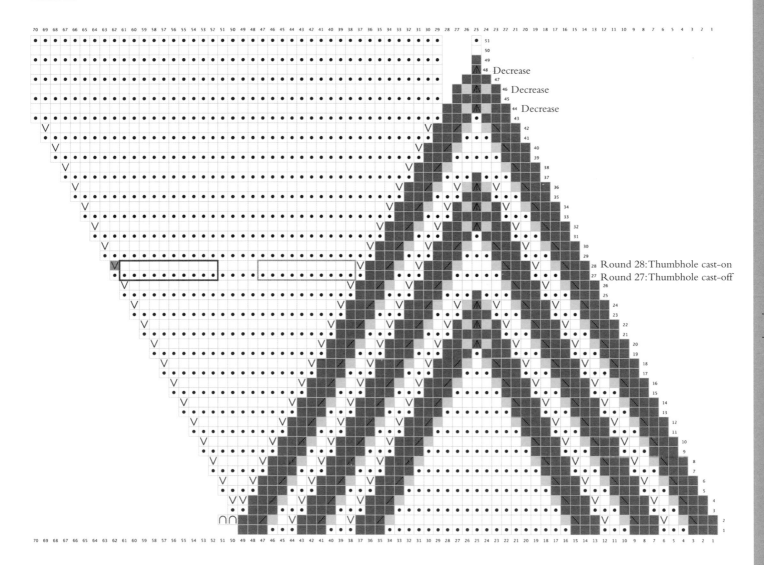

Decrease
Decrease
Decrease

Round 28: Thumbhole cast-on
Round 27: Thumbhole cast-off

cuff.

key.

■ Worked with Yarn B only, with Yarn A held at back	V splitA&B	∩ lifted increase, work first one as left-leaning and second as right-leaning
□ Worked with Yarn A&B held together	Y M1R	□ Right Thumbhole
□ knit	\ ssk	□ Left Thumbhole
• purl	▨ no stitch	/Λ sk2po
□ Cuff repeat	/ k2tog	▨ Work as kfb with Yarn A&B on left mitt ONLY
Y M1L		

size L.

hand.

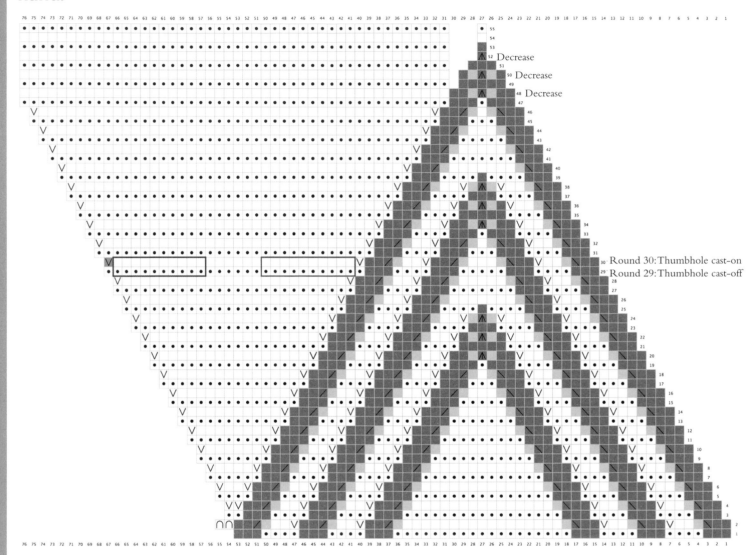

Round 30: Thumbhole cast-on
Round 29: Thumbhole cast-off

Decrease
Decrease
Decrease

cuff.

key.

▨	Worked with Yarn B only, with Yarn A held at back
☐	Worked with Yarn A&B held together
☐	knit
•	purl
☐	Cuff repeat
Y	M1L

V	splitA&B
⋎	M1R
\	ssk
▨	no stitch
/	k2tog
∩	lifted increase, work first one as left-leaning and second as right-leaning

☐	Right Thumbhole
☐	Left Thumbhole
⋀	sk2po
▨	Work as kfb with Yarn A&B on left mitt ONLY

When I was little, hot cross buns appeared in bakeries for only a brief window of time in the spring, somewhere around Easter. I used to fastidiously pick out every last little glistening square of candied citrus peel in disgust, while relishing the sweet, plump, golden-brown sultanas and squishy raisins (and even the suspiciously crunchy currants and the weirdly hardened edges of the white cross). Now, hot cross buns can be found year-round and I'm happy to enjoy the peel in situ. And like giant, sharing-sized, uncrossed hot cross buns, once-exotic panettone has become easy to come by, appearing in shops around New Year's to satisfy similar flavour cravings. In a reverse of hot cross buns' rise, hedgehogs are now much more scarce. A nonsense word, Hozkwoz combines a lispy version of 'hot-crossed' with a prickly touch of 'hedgehog'. These odd, beautiful creatures were once a frequent sight even in London, ambling around on their surprisingly long legs (or more likely squashed flat in the road). Times change.

In general, knitting stopped being taught in schools in the UK in the 1970s, as part of a push for a version of equality we largely still subscribe to, based on girls doing boys' things, but not the other way around. There's no denying this shift gave young women access to many subjects they had been barred from or had received little encouragement to study previously. However, it was done in a way that further demeaned and dismissed mending, cooking, sewing and knitting, by largely removing them from the curriculum in favour of science and maths. It seems like a painfully missed opportunity to celebrate the validity of a wider range of useful skills. This has led directly into our current predicament, where most people in the UK feel unable to make or mend things for themselves — survival skills. Many kids today may not have either a parent or grandparent who knows how to knit.

Around five years ago, I did a number of knitting projects in secondary schools. The students and I made site-specific art projects that involved knitting. On the first day of meeting the students, I liked to start off by asking what they thought about knitting. It let me gauge the crowd and got the conversational ball rolling. The usual responses were variations on 'it's for old people' and 'only grannies do it', tellingly paired with 'it's boring'. I was happy to allow the young people a chance to be a little insulting while venting their ambivalence at having a stranger come in to do something 'weird'. It also exposed their prejudices and set a benchmark for their teachers — how much would I change their opinions by the end of the project? It allowed me to ask them if it were possible that only old women could do it, because not many people know how; because it was something they weren't taught, something they weren't allowed or encouraged to learn. It's one thing to not like something you have tried, but quite something else to dismiss something you haven't. I wonder if I went into a school again now, whether knitting would be quite as unfamiliar and associated so particularly with older women.

yarn pairing notes.

The hedgehoggly-sounding nature of Hozkwoz deserved a couple more happy animal-related references and so this pattern is knitted in a combination of Baa Ram Ewe's Dovestone Natural Aran and Rusty Ferret's Polwarth. 'Baa-ram-ewe! Baa-ram-ewe! To your breed, your fleece, your clan be true! Sheep be true! Baa-ram-ewe!' is the Sheep Password used in Babe, the film based on Dick King-Smith's book *The Sheep-Pig*, about a piglet who takes on the role of a sheepdog. Because of that, it is also the name of the wonderful yarn shop in Leeds, Yorkshire, for whom Dovestone Natural Aran is spun. It comes in a range of eight undyed shades: five solids and

three marls. It is lovely and soft, thanks to the worsted spin and the combination of Blue-faced Leicester with Masham and Wensleydale to give it a gently hairy halo.

Rusty Ferret is the dyeing arm of Fluph in Dundee, Scotland. Naming Fluph took its proprietress, Leona Page, a long long time of careful consideration (aka, agonising), so she swore that when it came to naming her next business, she would take a quick and easy approach. Rusty Ferret was her partner's suggestion, in response to an interaction they had with an online gamer called Cosmic Badger Jam, which had sparked Leona's desire for a totally random name. I was drawn to using Rusty Ferret's Polwarth base, because I know Leona's honeymoon travels will take her to New Zealand, where the wool that was spun into this plump, round yarn is from. The Polwarth breed was originally developed next door, in Australia, for both good fleece and meat production, and proved hardier than their Merino cousins. It is easy to imagine they are handsome beasts, because you'd be excused for confusing Polwarth and Poldark.

construction and fit.

This hat is super squooshy and warm, thanks to mostly being in bouncy garter stitch using two lofty yarns held together. It is worked in quarters from the top down, in the round, starting with a pinhole cast-on, a circular method essential to add to your cast-on arsenal if you don't already have one. It's useful for toe-up socks, shawls that start in the centre and Pinglewins too. All of the shaping is worked at the crown. Garter stitch in the round requires alternating rounds of knit and purl, which would ordinarily form a visible 'seam' at the beginning of the round where you change from knit to purl and back again to start the following round. Here, however, the jog at the beginning of the round is masked by directly knitting the first single-coloured, 3-st stripe (of four) that extends down from the cross at the top of the hat and interrupts the garter stitch. Once all increases have been made on the crown, you work the body of the hat straight down, until the subtle decorative ribbing at the brim. The Reverse Broken Rib uses what is usually the wrong side of Broken Rib as the right side (hence 'reverse' in the name) to blend in better with the garter stitch than regular Broken Rib would. With a change back to the smaller needles you started the hat on, the rib brings the brim in just a little, to ensure a sleek look and better fit. You need to make sure to use an exceptionally stretchy cast-off that works with 1x1 ribbing, as the fit of the hat could easily be dictated by a too-tight brim, which would work against all the lovely stretchy stitches you have created for a snugly fitting hat.

sizing.

S (M, L)
Designed to be worn with approximately 4cm/1½" negative ease around forehead.

yarn.

Yarn A: Baa Ram Ewe, Dovestone Natural
(aran/worsted; 50% Bluefaced Leicester, 25% Wensleydale, 25% Masham; 170m/186yds per 100g/3½oz)
Natural No. 2 or 3 x 1

Yarn B: Rusty Ferret, Polwarth (DK/light worsted;
100% Polwarth (machine washable); 225m/246yds per 100g/3½oz)
Bru'd Fae Girders or Eldritch x 1

You will likely have enough Yarn B for a second hat in all sizes, but not Yarn A. If you are substituting yarns, you can stick with a DK/light worsted and aran/worsted combination. Alternatively, you can look for a sport and DK/light worsted or two DK/light worsteds to achieve a less dense fabric at the same gauge, thus still being able to follow the instructions without needing to adapt them. This will change the character of the hat a little. In the specified combination of yarns, the hat has been designed to have good structure: not quite a pill-box hat in sturdiness, but certainly not slouchy. In a different combination of lighter yarns at the specified gauge, the hat will have more drape.

gauge.

15 stitches x 32 rounds = 10cm x 10cm/4" x 4" over garter stitch with both yarns held together on larger needles after blocking.

Hozkwoz crown square 72 (80, 88) sts x 16 (18, 20) rounds = 12cm x 12cm/4¾" x 4¾" (14cm x 14cm/5½" x 5½", 16cm x 16cm/6¼" x 6¼") measuring the Yarn A cross (diagonally placed on the square) after blocking.

Swatching note: As this hat is worked from the top down (from the Crown to the Ribbed Brim), instead of working a separate swatch, you will get a more accurate idea of gauge (and construction) if you follow the instructions from the beginning of the pattern to the end of the Crown Shaping Increases (for your chosen size). For the truest gauge, with sts safely on hold (left live), soak, block and dry your Crown square/swatch, then measure the length of the Yarn A cross that runs on a diagonal to the square to see how it compares to the measurements given. If you are happy with your gauge, you can slide your sts back into action and continue on with your hat. If not, this was only meant to be a swatch; try again with a larger or smaller needle size and the satisfaction of having practised the construction. Leave your first experiment intact for now, so that you can compare and contrast.

notions.

tapestry needle
stitch marker

worn by...

Anna in Natural 2 and Bru'd Fae Girders, size M, knitted by Rachel Rawlins. The pink and orange dress is sewn (and dyed) by Marilla Walker from her Isca pattern.
Adam in Natural 3 and Eldritch, size M, knitted by Vonnie Williams.

needles.

4.5mm (US7) for start of Crown and Ribbed Brim.
5.5mm (US9) for Body.
4.5mm (US7) crochet hook for easier working of pinhole cast-on.

Always use a needle size that will result in the correct gauge after blocking.

Needle type note: This hat is worked top down in quarters. The Crown is square, with sets of instructions repeated 4 times each round. This makes it convenient for keeping track of stitches, especially while you are working the increases at the crown, if you use a set of 5 DPNs (rather than 4). This way, each quarter of the total number of sts gets its own needle (and you have one remaining needle to work with). You can always transfer on to 40cm/16" length circular needles after working the crown. If magic-looping is more your jam, you may wish to use 4 markers to note where each quarter starts and ends.

glossary.

REVERSE BROKEN RIB
(worked in the round over 3 DS sts and a multiple of 2 sts + 1)
Round 1: ★K3A for DS, [pA&B] to next DS★, repeat from ★ to ★ to end.
Round 2: ★K3A for DS, k1A&B, [p1A&B, k1A&B] to next DS★, repeat from ★ to ★ to end.

splitA&B
Using Yarn A&B held together, knit into the Yarn A and Yarn B sections of next stitch individually, as if they were 2 separate stitches. 1-st increase.

pattern notes.

When forming the yarn overs (yo) in Crown Shaping Rounds 1 and 4, work them the short way, by bringing the yarn from the WS to the RS between the needle tips, as if to purl, and then knit the next st: the action of knitting the next st from this position will return the yarn from front to back to form the yo. This makes for a nice, centrally placed inc.

In Rounds 2 and 5, incs are worked as a knit front and back (kfb) through the back loop (tbl) into the yo you made in the previous round. By working the inc into the back leg of the yo, you avoid a hole forming. This could be written as 'kbf' (knit back and front) into yo, but 'kbf' look so similar to 'kfb' (knit front and back), that it could get confusing, so the longer 'kfb tbl' has been used, even though you are working the 'kfb' part in reverse order.

schematic.

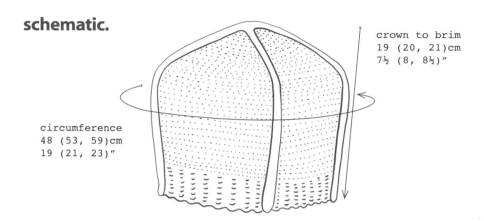

crown to brim
19 (20, 21)cm
7½ (8, 8½)"

circumference
48 (53, 59)cm
19 (21, 23)"

pattern begins.

Using a crochet hook, Yarn A and the pinhole method, aka Emily Ocker's circular cast–on, cast on 8 sts. Transfer sts to spread evenly across smaller needles. PM to mark BOR.

crown shaping increases.

Round 1 (inc): [K2, yo] to end. (4 sts inc) *12 sts*

Round 2 (inc): [K2, kfb tbl into yo from previous round] to end. (4 sts inc) *16 sts*

Introduce Yarn B.

Round 3: [K3A, p1A&B] to end.

Round 4 (inc): [K3A, yoA&B, k1A&B] to end. (4 sts inc) *20 sts*

Round 5 (inc): [K3A, kfb tblA&B into yo from previous round, p1A&B] to end. (4 sts inc) *24 sts*

Round 6: [K3A, p3A&B] to end.

Change to larger needles.

Round 7 (inc): [K3A, splitA&B, k1A&B, splitA&B] to end. (8 sts inc) *32 sts*

Round 8: [K3A, p5A&B] to end.

Round 9 (inc): ★K3A, [splitA&B] x 2, k1A&B, [splitA&B] x 2★ repeat from ★ to ★ to end. (16 sts inc) *48 sts*

Round 10: [K3A, p9A&B] to end.

Round 11 (inc): [K3A, splitA&B, k7A&B, splitA&B] to end. (8 sts inc) *56 sts*

Round 12: [K3A, p11A&B] to end.

Round 13 (inc): [K3A, splitA&B, k9A&B, splitA&B] to end. (8 sts inc) *64 sts*

Round 14: [K3A, p13A&B] to end.

Round 15 (inc): [K3A, splitA&B, k11A&B, splitA&B] to end. (8 sts inc) *72 sts*

Round 16: [K3A, p15A&B] to end.

Increases for size S are complete. Time to work the Body for this size.

Sizes M and L only

Round 17 (inc): [K3A, splitA&B, k13A&B, splitA&B] to end. (8 sts inc) *80 sts*

Round 18: [K3A, p17A&B] to end.

Increases for size M are complete. Time to work the Body for this size.

Size L only
Round 19 (inc): [K3A, splitA&B, k15A&B, splitA&B] to end.
(8 sts inc) *88 sts*
Round 20: [K3A, p19A&B] to end.

Increases for size L are complete. Time to work the Body for this size.

all sizes again.
72 (80, 88) sts

body.
Maintain the four 3-st Yarn A DS in st st, as set, until you cast off, regardless of what you do in the Yarn A&B quarters between them.

Starting with a knit round, work in garter stitch for 35 (37, 39) more rounds, ending with a knit round. This will form 17 (18, 19) garter ridges. Your hat should currently measure 15.5 (17, 18) cm/6 (6¾, 7)" from cast-on.

ribbed brim.
Change to smaller needles.

Work in Reverse Garter Rib for 10 rounds (see Glossary).

Making sure to use a really stretchy cast-off method suitable for 1x1 rib for the Yarn A&B sections, cast off as follows:
K3A for DS catching Yarn B float behind 2nd st,
★[k1A&B, p1A&B] to 1 st before next DS, then, to keep pattern consistent and not interrupt the DS, k4A catching Yarn B float behind 2nd st★. Repeat from ★ to ★ twice more, [k1A&B, p1A&B] to last st. Knit final st with Yarn A only.

special finishing instructions.
After a soak and squeeze-out of excess water, allow to dry over a balloon inflated to slightly smaller than head size, or flat, divided down the centre of a DS on each side. See General Finishing Instructions on page 142 for additional guidance.

/ˈgɪŋnam/

GINGNAM

A gingham-style knitted fabric just had to be called Gingnam — to conjure up the K-pop sound and signature dance of Psy's 2012 hit, *Gangnam Style*, which saw him throwing moves a bit like riding a horse (which ties in nicely with the old-fashioned associations of gingham). Though the tunes haven't drawn me in, I am intrigued by K-pop (Korean pop music): without being classified as 'world music', it has garnered a devoted fan base in music markets usually dominated by tracks produced in the western hemisphere. Who knows, perhaps one day it will start to tickle me.

My Oma had a theory that your taste changes every seven years. I relate this to the fact I learned much later that it apparently takes the human body seven years to completely replace every cell. Holding on to a rule his mother instilled in him to try everything at least twice, I know a guy who retries food he doesn't enjoy every couple of years to see if he feels differently. Because of my Oma, I have tried to like the act of weaving on many occasions. I appreciate the results of the process and know many wonderful people who would describe themselves as weavers. So far, the thrill eludes me. I think it is the fact that so many decisions need to be made in advance and then committed to with the warp before the really touchy-feely colourful part starts. When knitting, I like that I can change my mind at any point and deviate from the plan — my plan. Admittedly, these different emotions are in part down to my comparative levels of skill in the two disciplines, but my response is also based on the linear grid of weave and the looping nature of knit. When weaving, you make fabric; when knitting, you make the thing.

I would like to like to weave. It was my Oma's profession and I grew up playing under and around her loom. Though she hasn't been alive for many years now, friends and family still rock clothing made by her from fabrics that she wove. She was multicraftual, and sometimes the bodies of the jackets for which she had woven the fabric would have knitted sleeves added, often in yarn she had spun. Though I am not (yet) a weaver, she remains a major influence and I love knowing that, though neither my mother or I have seriously taken to weaving, she directly led friends my mother grew up with to become weavers. And the thing is, when I look at these patterns and the whole concept of Marlisle, I very much see my Oma's presence. The way the colours combine is distinctly akin to weaving, in a way handknitting usually can't achieve.

yarn pairing notes.

Though the Gotland breed of sheep originates in the region of Sweden from which it gets its name, the long-haired beauties that produced the fleece for the yarn used in this pattern are raised by Emma Boyles on Well Manor Farm in the southern English county of Hampshire where it borders Surrey. She works closely with the shepherd Susie Parish (and her sheepdogs, Nan, Joe and Lad). Between them, this dynamic duo make sure that both the domesticated and wild animals that share the land they farm are well cared for and that the farm's soil is maintained for future generations. I've met few people so intimately involved in the whole process of raising sheep and creating yarn. For her Gotland yarn, Emma makes sure only the best parts of the long-locked fleece are selected to send west to

John Arbon's mill in Devon to be worsted-spun into a glossy, exceptionally warm yarn with a good halo. If you've ever encountered The Little Grey Sheep booth at a yarn show, you will have seen the carefully displayed yarns (dyed by Emma) on a specially designed stand that never looks messy, as each skein has its own hook to hang from. Emma and Susie have even developed a new breed of sheep, the Stein, bred for softness of yarn in an era when most sheep are raised for high yield of meat and lamb production.

In keeping with the Scandinavian heritage of the Gotland breed used in The Little Grey Sheep yarn, I've paired it with Dandelion Yarns, which is dyed in Stockholm, Sweden. In my mind, Anna 'Dandelion' Strandberg is the Queen of Mint. I have a feeling she would happily dye only greens and blues, eschewing all other colours, if she could. She dyes on super-soft and consistent Rosy Green Wool produced by Rosy Stegmann and Patrick Gruban in Munich, Germany, out of fleece from Merino sheep raised in Patagonia, Argentina, and spun at the Natural Fibre Company mill in Cornwall, UK. Yarn from Rosy Green Wool undertakes this zig-zagging journey as these are the circuitous steps it needs to go through in order to be classified as GOTS (Global Organic Textile Standard), the highest form of organic certification for textiles, which guarantees that human beings, not only animals and the land, are looked after every step of the way. It is one of the very few GOTS-certified yarns available. The system of certification came about because there are no legal parameters around using the term 'organic' and it was felt that a system should be in place to prove and classify how rigorously certain companies adhere to the ethos. Such processes are not easy or cheap to institute and verify, and so it currently requires this geographic spread of places that have met those stringent standards. Also interesting to note is that this yarn has gone through an unusual process that makes it machine-washable without the use of the standard chlorine or other harsh chemicals involved in regular superwash treatments. This means that this yarn is watertight, Happy Yarn.

Local, traceable, transparent, ethical, fair-trade, cruelty-free, organic and eco are not mutually exclusive, it is often necessary to chose which to prioritise. If I am honest, I had shied away from using a yarn with so many geographic steps and processes involved. The majority of the book's recommended yarns come straight from the farmers who rear the sheep that produce the fleece spun into yarn, or from dyers who use yarn from farms and mills local to them. This neighbourly knowledge and investment creates situations where all involved feel happy about the ethics and environmental impacts of the processes involved. There is a high level of trust that bypasses the need for certification as they are linked by the bonds of local knowledge and ongoing proximity. But many do not have a certificate that verifies their 'goodness'.

Perhaps even more than the neat Swedish connection, this idea of what constitutes a Happy Yarn is at the crux of this pairing. The two yarns used in this pattern beautifully illustrate two of the different ways this can be achieved — if you know the people and a farm well, you can make your own decisions and if you don't, there's certification that can stand in for personal knowledge. One hairy and one super-smooth, both soft and with a conscience in their own ways. Yarns you can feel deeply happy about what your use of them supports.

construction and fit.

Gingnam is an excellent entry point into Marlisle and shows off the hallmarks of imperceptible round changes and use of just two colours to make patterns that would usually require three. The suggested yarns are two different weights: an aran and a sport weight used in combination. The difference in the weight of the yarns and structure of the single-yarn stocking-stitch rectangles neighbouring garter-stitch rectangles using both yarns held together will naturally force the single-colour rectangles into a slight hourglass shape as part of the intentional character of the knit.

For an idea of which size to chose, guidance is given about how it is intended to fit around the ears, as these are likely to be the widest point of your head and neck. From this, you can ascertain whether you would like a snug or wide-fitting cowl. By offering a range of sizes, it makes it easy to substitute different yarn weights (if you're prepared to play around with finding the correct gauge for your chosen yarn combo). Generally, if you use thinner yarn, use smaller needles and the instructions for the larger size. If you use thicker yarn, use bigger needles and the smaller cowl size instructions.

The cowl can be worked up longer, bearing in mind this will use more yarn and obscure the stitch pattern in the folds you will create. Extensive notes are given on how to work extra repeats. Alternatively, if you're up for more of a challenge and know you have extra yarn, you could double-knit the single-colour rectangles using the yarn that would otherwise be the float across the back — one colour on one side and the other on the reverse. This would make it a truly reversible pattern. A cowl doesn't need to be reversible, but just imagine the satisfaction, and this then opens up the possibility of using the same stitch structure for a baby blanket or scarf. You could even work it flat in that case.

Perhaps the simplest pattern in the collection, this cowl is easy yet striking, and satisfying to work in the round in two colours of yarn with a good contrast.

sizing.

S (M, L)

Designed to be worn with 5cm/2" positive ease, when measuring head around ears.

yarn.

Yarn A: The Little Grey Sheep, British Gotland Aran (aran/worsted; 100% Gotland; 176m/192yds per 100g/3½oz) Natural x 1

Yarn B: Dandelion Yarns, Dandelion Rosy Sport (sport; 100% organic Merino (machine washable); 320m/350yds per 100g/3½oz) Iceberg or Blue Jean x 1

Note: This pattern can work with an alternative two different weights of yarn in combination or two same-weight yarns together. You will need to adjust your gauge and needle size accordingly and the dimensions of the cowl will change. When combining different weights, they should be close, for example, when you stash dive, keep an eye out for a DK/light worsted and an aran/worsted to combine, or a sport and a DK to use together. A sport and a 4ply/fingering will give you a more petite check (and a significantly smaller cowl, so you should use the instructions for size L).

worn by...

Anna in Natural and Blue Jean, size M (with extra repeat), knitted by Mandy Hewett. The pink coat is sewn by Marilla Walker from her Honetone pattern, and just visible is the yellow dress from her Isca pattern.

Adam in Natural and Iceberg, size M (standard length), knitted by Anna Maltz.

gauge.

20 stitches x 30 rounds = 10cm x 10cm/4" x 4" over Gingnam stitch pattern after blocking.

Note: A slightly looser stitch gauge will work fine, but not tighter or the denser aran/worsted Yarn A rectangles will start to buckle. Alternatively, if you get too loose, the Yarn B rectangles will start to look flimsy in comparison. Round gauge is of less importance, though may result in the use of more or less yarn.

needles.

4.5mm (US7) circular needles, 40cm/16" long. If making size M or L sts may fit more easily on a 60cm/24" needle.

Always use a needle size that will result in the correct gauge after blocking.

notions.

tapestry needle
stitch marker

glossary.

GINGNAM REPEAT

(worked in the round over a multiple of 10 sts)

Round 1: [K5A&B, k5A] to end.
Round 2: [P5A&B, k5A] to end.
Rounds 3-8: Repeat Rounds 1-2.
Round 9: [K5B, k5A&B] to end.
Round 10: [K5B, p5A&B] to end.
Rounds 11-16: Repeat Rounds 9-10.

pattern notes.

Floats: The floats at the back of this cowl span 5 sts. On the first and last rounds of the cowl only, catch the Yarn B float behind the Yarn A st from Column 8 of every repeat, as instructed, to stop floats popping out and showing on the RS. Catching your float is unnecessary the remainder of the time and might interfere with the clarity of the colour on the front (and slow you down). If you feel you really must catch your floats, then make sure to vary where you catch them, to minimise how much they show up on the RS.

Total reversibility: If you enjoy a little extra challenge and want to do away with floats entirely, this specific stitch structure lends itself well to becoming a totally reversible fabric if you double-knit the single-colour squares using the specified colour on the RS and the other colour (that would be the floats) on the WS. The garter sts in both colours in the square below means that you are already set up for using 2 sets of stitches. This approach will take extra yarn.

Working extra repeats: With the specified yarns and gauge, you can safely work 5 full 16-round repeats when working a size S, before finishing with a final half repeat for a deeper, 30cm/11¾" cowl. For sizes M and L you work only 4 full 16-round repeats for a shallower, 24cm/9½" cowl. If you are prepared to play yarn chicken, you should just be able to get the 5½ repeats in size M for a deeper cowl. There will not be enough Yarn A to make the deeper size L.

If you substitute yarns, depending on the meterage, you can work as many repeats of the pattern as you fancy and your yarn allows, casting off as instructed after working a Round 7 of a final half repeat (for symmetry with the start of the cowl). This may mean guesstimating whether you have enough yarn to work the number of repeats you desire before you start that extra one. If guesstimating isn't your style, you can weigh your yarn before you start the cowl and after your first repeat. If you subtract the weight of the leftover yarn from the original weight, you are left with the weight of a single repeat. When you have worked a safe number of repeats, you can weigh the yarn you have left over to see if you have enough for one more.

schematic.

depth
30 (24/30, 24)cm
11¾ (9½/11½, 9½)"

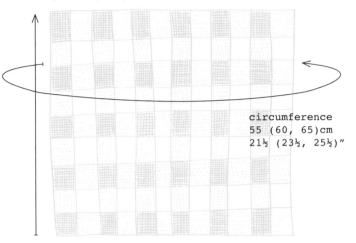

circumference
55 (60, 65)cm
21½ (23½, 25½)"

pattern begins.

Using Yarn A and the long-tail method, cast on 110 (120, 130) sts. Join in the round, being careful not to twist. PM to mark BOR.

Working from Gingnam Repeat chart or written instructions (see Glossary), work the 10-st repeat 11 (12, 13) times across the round, catching the Yarn B float behind the Yarn A st from Column 8 of each repeat in Round 1 only.

Continue as set, working to end of 16-round repeat 5 (4, 4) times, then work Rounds 1-6 of chart or written instructions only once more. Work a final Round 7 to finish, catching the Yarn B float behind the Yarn A st from Column 8 of each repeat.

Break Yarn B, leaving a tail long enough to sew in later.

Cast off using Yarn A only, purling the purl sts and knitting the knit stitches (as for Round 8) as you cast them off, otherwise the WS will show on the RS. See General Finishing Instructions on page 142 for guidance on what to do now.

gingnam repeat.

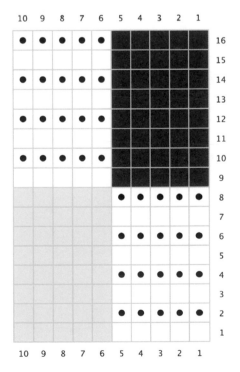

key.

☐	Worked with Yarn A&B held together
▨	Knit with Yarn A only, with Yarn B held at back
■	Knit with Yarn B only, with Yarn A held at back
☐	knit
●	purl

SHANTAY

/ˈʃanteɪ/

During the design process, this cardigan has gone by many different names. First was Crocodile Tongues, because the gently pink Viola colourway used is called Giant Peach. The stories of Roald Dahl helped shape the childhoods of many of us who grew up into playful, inquisitive and forthright adults with a sense of responsibility to navigate through what we are dealt with humour and care. Crocodile tongues were the magic bean that made the peach and its insect inhabitants grow to gargantuan proportions so they could be the same size as James, the little boy, and help him escape his terrible aunts to go on an adventure to New York City. With a little further research, I learned that crocodiles have the peculiarity of not being able to move their tongues, a fact that has been added to my list of animal soundbites that includes armadillos always having identical quadruplets (and carrying leprosy) and that cats are the only animal to have voluntarily domesticated themselves. Crocodile Tongues got shortened to CT during the tech-editing process, because it was a bit of a mouthful and we were scanning for problems, just as a CT scan would do.

The next idea was to call it Perzik — Dutch for peach, with a cool 'k' at the end, like Drazik, the bad boy of the 90s TV series Heartbreak High. Then, through the test and sample-knitting phase it went by Zazie. I've been the resident columnist at Pom Pom Quarterly for a good while now and occasionally contribute patterns. This stitch pattern was first cooked up for a cowl in the 5th-anniversary edition of the magazine. It was named Zazie, after the feisty girl on the Métro of French New Wave cinema (based on the book by Raymond Queneau). I fell in love with the stitch structure so much that I wanted to do more with it, and this cardigan is the result.

Still, in trying to come up with a name that wasn't already on Ravelry and that rolled off the tongue a little more, this cardigan finally became Shantay. While I enjoy being a trendsetter in certain areas of life, my television-watching habits aren't one of them. I'm generally slow to the game, waiting until I am so intrigued by everyone's rave reviews that I have to see what the fuss is all about and work out a way to watch it. We don't have a telly in our small flat or a telly licence. A good seven years late to the game, I've been catching up with RuPaul's Drag Race. I am not one for the overt bitchiness and competition, but I appreciate the ways that drag celebrates the joy of dressing up, creating your own all-encompassing look that reflects more than just aesthetics, and giving a finger to the dominant hegemony. Those things are all part of the reason I knit. And Shantay (a non-dictionary word, abbreviated from the French *enchanté*, that forms part of a RuPaul catchphrase as a counter-point to sashay) shares a 'shhhhhhhh' sound with Chanel jacket, of which the boxy shape, dense knit and marled surface of this cardigan are reminiscent.

What unites all these characters — those of Roald Dahl, Drazik, Zazie, RuPaul (and her drag queens) and Coco Chanel herself, is that they all are passionate, feisty, have edge, push boundaries and are considered deviant by other people's standards. This cardigan is certainly no simpering, run-of-the-mill, easy knit. So there you go, Shantay, you stay.

yarn pairing notes.

Ontario, an eastern province of Canada, and the south-western English county of Devon are far apart as the crow flies, yet are united by a bond of friendship between Emily Foden of Viola, the hand-dyed yarn brand, and Juliet Sensicle and John Arbon of John Arbon Textiles. Emily worked with John and Juliet at their mill in Devon for three years from 2012. That's why you'll find John Arbon has a range of dry-dyed yarns (where the colour is added to the carded and washed fleece before it is spun, rather than after) called Viola, developed with them by Emily.

In Emily's shop, you'll find that a number of the bases she dyes on are spun especially for her by the Arbon mill. With so many overlaps, it would have made sense to use a combo of Viola from John Arbon Textiles and one of Emily's bases spun at the Arbon mill, but it seemed nice to add extra diversity and reflect the place where Emily is now (as well as the fact that, to stick to my own rules, I needed one dyed and one undyed yarn for this pairing). She lives and dyes in Mooresburg, a small village in Amish country, in what was once the general store. The fleece for the yarn is gathered from her neighbours' Cotswold/Dorset cross flock. Her Mooresburg DK base is spun for her in nearby Wellington County at a small family-run mill where they are passionate about local fibres and raise Angora goats in the surrounding fields. In a wonderful woolly world sort of way, when Donna Hancock of Wellington Fibres attended the Yorkshire yarn festival of Yarndale this year, she introduced herself to John, being curious about his mill. When he worked out that she was Canadian, he asked her if she knew Emily Foden and of course, she did!

John and Juliet are central characters in the UK yarn scene for the yarns they spin for them-selves and for others. Dear to me both for their really can-do attitude and sense of fun — hearing Juliet laugh is a treat to be experienced at the best UK yarn festivals and if you are additionally lucky, you might get to dance to John doing a DJ set. The Zwartbles sheep breed is especially close to their hearts and raised more locally than some of the other wools and fibres they spin. It's also a breed that originates in The Netherlands, which has neat personal relevance to me, as so do half my family. Because Zwart-bles are a dark-brown breed, their fleece is then mixed with varying amounts of Exmoor Blueface to create the three shades of natural, undyed grey that make up this specific range of sweet-smelling, DK/light worsted yarn.

construction and fit.

As a truly all-over cardigan, Shantay's zigzag pattern is only interrupted by intentional garter-stitch button bands and the gussets that run under the arms on the full-length, tapered sleeves to avoid needing to work increases directly into the flow of the zigzags. There is no shaping in the body, but there are short rows concealed in the zigzags of the yoke to raise the back and give the generous round neckline a scoop at the front. Decreases are spread across the circumference of the yoke. The stitch structure contains enough garter stitch to make it lie flat, so no special edging (such as moss stitch or ribbing) is needed.

Shantay includes a steek in the centre of the front, so that the body and yoke of the cardigan can be worked seamlessly in the round. Instructions are given for a knotted steek. Other methods could easily be substituted, if you have a familiar favourite or another you were itching to try. The knotted steek, also used in the Ess Shawl (page 84) and Ruperto Scarf (page 110) to create a fringed edge, is used here because it sits beautifully flat and doesn't interrupt the zigzag pattern on the front or affect the natural stretch of the knitted fabric. I suggest you cut the steek in silence, so you can hear the beautiful snipping sound clearly. After casting off the neckline and cutting the steek, the garter-stitch button bands are picked up and knitted from the knotted steek edge. The final step is sewing in the steek ends before blocking and adding buttons.

Made by your own fair hands, wear it as an outer layer and channel the classic Chanel jacket.

schematic.

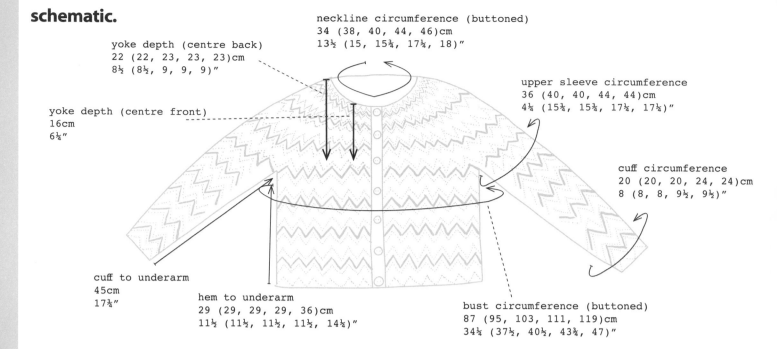

neckline circumference (buttoned)
34 (38, 40, 44, 46)cm
13½ (15, 15¾, 17¼, 18)"

yoke depth (centre back)
22 (22, 23, 23, 23)cm
8½ (8½, 9, 9, 9)"

yoke depth (centre front)
16cm
6¼"

upper sleeve circumference
36 (40, 40, 44, 44)cm
4¼ (15¾, 15¾, 17¼, 17¼)"

cuff circumference
20 (20, 20, 24, 24)cm
8 (8, 8, 9½, 9½)"

cuff to underarm
45cm
17¾"

hem to underarm
29 (29, 29, 29, 36)cm
11½ (11½, 11½, 11½, 14¼)"

bust circumference (buttoned)
87 (95, 103, 111, 119)cm
34¼ (37½, 40½, 43¾, 47)"

sizing.

XS (S, M, L, XL)
Designed to be worn with 5-7.5cm/2-3" positive ease around bust. If you are on the fence about which size to work, opt for the smaller of the two.

yarn.

Yarn A: John Arbon, Zwartbles (DK/light worsted; 60% Zwartbles, 40% Exmoor Blueface; 250m/273yds per 100g/3½oz) Mid x 4 (4, 4, 5, 5)

Yarn B: Viola, Mooresburg DK (DK/light worsted; 100% Ontario Cotswold/Dorset cross; 238m/260yds per 100g/3½oz) Giant Peach or Muscari x 4 (4, 4, 5, 5)

worn by...

Vonnie in Mid and Muscari, size M, knitted by Debbie Muir. The mint coat is sewn by Marilla Walker from her Honetone pattern, and the chambray dress from her Isca pattern.
Marilla in Mid and Giant Peach, size L, knitted by Anna Maltz. The grey splatter-dyed dress is sewn (and dyed) by Marilla Walker from her Isca pattern.

Note: Marilla would ordinarily wear a size M, but the pink and grey sample is a size L, so that's what she wore.

gauge.

20 stitches x 34 rounds = 10cm x 10cm/4" x 4" over Shantay V stitch pattern after blocking.

Gauge warning: Your round gauge is important for the fit of this pattern. If your round gauge varies more than 2 rounds either way (outside of the 32-36 rounds per 10cm/4"), you are likely to need to make adjustments to accommodate. The same goes for making adjustments for fit preference, such as longer/shorter Sleeves or Body. Because the cardigan has an all-over pattern, making adjustments is distinctly fiddly and long-winded, best broached only by the mathematically confident knitter.

Swatching note: Make a circular swatch working from Shantay V with at least 25 sts (3 times the 8-st repeat, plus a final st from Column 9). Alternatively, you can simply follow instructions from the start of Sleeve for your chosen size and work through the Cuff and a Round Repeat of the Main Sleeve, so it is at least 15cm/6". Wash and block it (with sts left live) before measuring. If you are satisfied with your gauge, continue on with the Sleeve, if not, it was a swatch, not a Sleeve. Don't unravel your swatch till you can compare it with your next Sleeve/swatch.

needles.

4mm (US6) circular needle for Body and Yoke at least 80cm/32" long. If making sizes L or XL, sts may fit more easily on a 100cm/40" needle.
4mm (US6) needles suitable for working small circumferences in the round for Sleeves and end of Yoke.

Always use a needle size that will result in the correct gauge after blocking.

Extra needle note: If you have the luxury of adding an extra set, it's easiest to have separate needles for each Sleeve (and for the Body).

notions.

tapestry needle
two locking stitch markers
smooth waste yarn or stitch holder for putting Underarm sts on hold
long, sharp needle with large eye, for sewing in steek ends
strong slippery thread for sewing up button band during blocking
7 (7, 7, 7, 8) 22mm/¾" diameter buttons

pattern notes.

Contrary to popular wisdom, don't read the whole pattern before starting: you'll freak yourself out. The instructions look way more complicated if you only read them without doing them. A lot of work, by many knitters, has gone into making them trustworthy. Once you start, if you focus on the section you are working, with the instructions at hand, you will be guided through each stage and it should quickly become intuitive.

The charts are named 'A' and 'V' because of the shape of the zig-zag you start and finish working your repeat with. 'A' is a triangle launching up like a rocket. It looks like a mountain peak whereas 'V' is a valley, more like an arrowhead, shooting into the ground.

glossary.

splitA&B
Using Yarn A&B held together, knit into the Yarn A and Yarn B sections of next stitch individually, as if they were 2 separate stitches. 1-st increase.

shantay A.

(worked over multiple of 8 sts + 1)

SET-UP ROUNDS
Set-up Round 1: [K1A, k7A&B] to last st, k1A.
Set-up Round 2: [K1A, p7A&B] to last st, k1A.

REPEAT ROUNDS
Round 1: [K2A, k5A&B, k1A] to last st, k1A.
Round 2: [K2A, p5A&B, k1A] to last st, k1A.
Round 3: [K3A, k3A&B, k2A] to last st, k1A.
Round 4: [K3A, p3A&B, k2A] to last st, k1A.
Round 5: [K1A&B, k3A, k1A&B, k3A] to last st, k1A&B.
Round 6: [P1A&B, k3A, p1A&B, k3A] to last st, p1A&B.
Round 7: [K2A&B, k5B, k1A&B] to last st, k1A&B.
Round 8: [P2A&B, k5B, p1A&B] to last st, p1A&B.
Round 9: [K3A&B, k3B, k2A&B] to last st, k1A&B.
Round 10: [P3A&B, k3B, p2A&B] to last st, p1A&B.
Round 11: [K1B, k3A&B, k1A, k3A&B] to last st, k1B.
Round 12: [K1B, p3A&B, k1A, p3A&B] to last st, k1B.
Round 13: [K2B, k5A&B, k1B] to last st, k1B.
Round 14: [K2B, p5A&B, k1B] to last st, k1B.
Round 15: [K3B, k3A&B, k2B] to last st, k1B.
Round 16: [K3B, p3A&B, k2B] to last st, k1B.
Round 17: [K1A&B, k3B, k1A&B, k3B] to last st, k1A&B.
Round 18: [P1A&B, k3B, p1A&B, k3B] to last st, p1A&B.
Round 19: [K2A&B, k5B, k1A&B] to last st, k1A&B.
Round 20: [P2A&B, k5B, p1A&B] to last st, p1A&B.
Round 21: [K3A&B, k3B, k2A&B] to last st, k1A&B.
Round 22: [P3A&B, k3B, p2A&B] to last st, p1A&B.
Round 23: [K1A, k3A&B, k1B, k3A&B] to last st, k1A.
Round 24: [K1A, p3A&B, k1B, p3A&B] to last st, k1A.

shantay V.

(worked over multiple of 8 sts + 1)

SET-UP ROUNDS
Set-up Round 1: [K4A&B, k1A, k3A&B] to last st, k1A&B.
Set-up Round 2: [P4A&B, k1A, p3A&B] to last st, p1A&B.

REPEAT ROUNDS
Round 1: [K3A&B, k3A, k2A&B] to last st, k1A&B.
Round 2: [P3A&B, k3A, p2A&B] to last st, p1A&B.
Round 3: [K2A&B, k5A, k1A&B] to last st, k1A&B.
Round 4: [P2A&B, k5A, p1A&B] to last st, p1A&B.
Round 5: [K1A&B, k3A, k1A&B, k3A] to last st, k1A&B.
Round 6: [P1A&B, k3A, p1A&B, k3A] to last st, p1A&B.
Round 7: [K3A, k3A&B, k2A] to last st, k1A.
Round 8: [K3A, p3A&B, k2A] to last st, k1A.
Round 9: [K2A, k5A&B, k1A] to last st, k1A.
Round 10: [K2A, p5A&B, k1A] to last st, k1A.
Round 11: [K1A, k3A&B, k1B, k3A&B] to last st, k1A.
Round 12: [K1A, p3A&B, k1B, p3A&B] to last st, k1A.
Round 13: [K3A&B, k3B, k2A&B] to last st, k1A&B.
Round 14: [P3A&B, k3B, p2A&B] to last st, p1A&B.
Round 15: [K2A&B, k5B, k1A&B] to last st, k1A&B.
Round 16: [P2A&B, k5B, p1A&B] to last st, p1A&B.
Round 17: [K1A&B, k3B, k1A&B, k3B] to last st, k1A&B.
Round 18: [P1A&B, k3B, p1A&B, k3B] to last st, p1A&B.
Round 19: [K3B, k3A&B, k2B] to last st, k1B.
Round 20: [K3B, p3A&B, k2B] to last st, k1B.
Round 21: [K2B, k5A&B, k1B] to last st, k1B.
Round 22: [K2B, p5A&B, k1B] to last st, k1B.
Round 23: [K1B, k3A&B, k1A, k3A&B] to last st, k1B.
Round 24: [K1B, p3A&B, k1A, p3A&B] to last st, k1B.

shantay A.

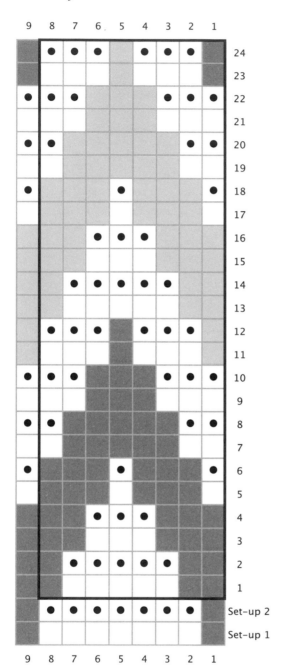

shantay shaping A.

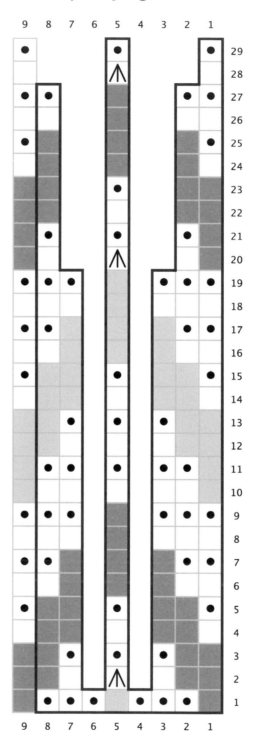

shantay V.

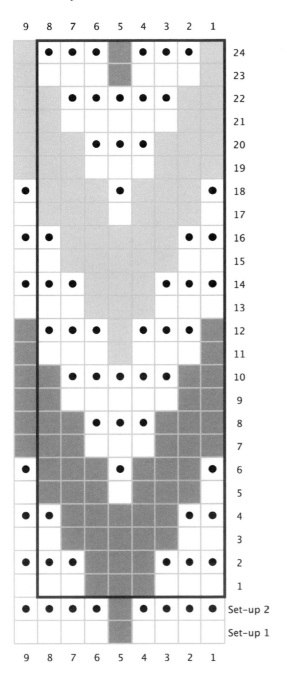

shantay shaping V.

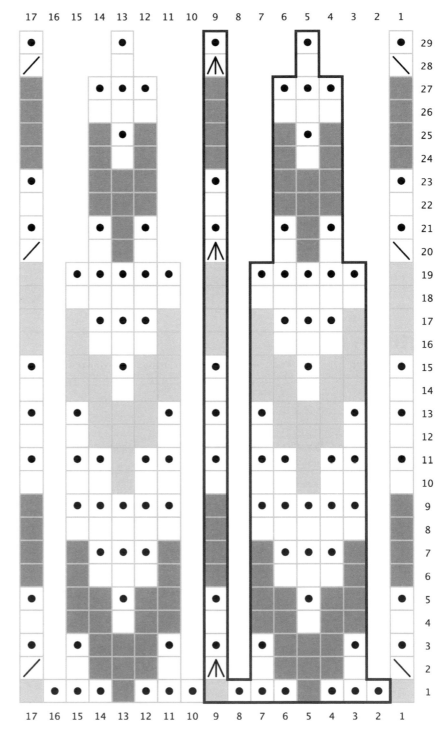

key.

	Worked with Yarn A only, with Yarn B held at back
	Worked with Yarn A&B held together
	Worked with Yarn B only, with Yarn A held at back

	knit
•	purl
	Repeat

⋀	CDD
╲	ssk
╱	k2tog

pattern begins.

sleeves.

Both sleeves worked alike, in the round, from Shantay V charted and written instructions.

Using Yarn A and needles suitable for working small circumferences in the round, and the long-tail method, cast on 40 (40, 40, 48, 48) sts. Join in the round being careful not to twist. PM to mark BOR.

cuff.

The Cuff is worked straight.
Garter Round 1:
Using Yarn A&B held together, knit to end of round.
Garter Round 2:
Using Yarn A&B held together, purl to end of round.

Set-up Round 1: Working from Set-up Row 1 of Shantay V chart, work boxed 8-st repeat 5 (5, 5, 6, 6) times across the round, ignoring st in Column 9 for now.

Set-up Round 1 sets placement of pattern. Work from Set-up Row 2, then Rows 1-23 of Shantay V as set, ignoring st in Column 9.

Note: From now on, when working Shantay V for the Sleeve you will only repeat Rows 1-24, NOT Set-up Rows 1-2.

main sleeve.

Size XS ONLY
Work Row 24 of Shantay V, ignoring st in Column 9.
Work Rows 1-23 of Shantay V again, ignoring st in Column 9.

all sizes again.

ESTABLISHING INCREASE GUSSET

Sleeve increases are worked under the arm in a garter-stitch gusset introduced between the beginning and end of the charted pattern. As increases are worked, the gusset grows, becoming a triangle of garter stitch pointing down to the wrist. Once you have 17 sts in the gusset, 16 sts are transferred out of the gusset and into the charted zone. These 16 sts allow 2 extra 8-st repeats of the chart to be worked in the charted zone (1 repeat to be worked at the beginning of the round and 1 repeat to be worked at the end) so that you only ever work full 8-st repeats in the charted zone. You then start a new gusset triangle extending up from the single remaining stitch in the centre of the gusset. Increases are worked along the edges of the new gusset in the same way you did in the previous one.

Round 1 (inc): Work 1 st from Column 1 from Row 24 of Shantay V, split A&B, continuing with Column 2 work rest of Row 24 of Shantay V as set, ignoring st in Column 9, split A&B, SM. (2 sts inc) *42 (42, 42, 50, 50) sts*

Note: Of the 2 sts increased, 1 st will become the gusset and the other st will become Column 9.

Round 2 (marker placement): P1A&B for gusset, PMX, work Row 1 of Shantay V as set (including Column 9 at the end to be worked after all the full 8-st repeats), SM (this marker is now MY)
Round 3 (partial): K1A&B for gusset. Round now starts here at MX.
Round 4: Work Row 2 of Shantay V (including Column 9 at the end to be worked after all the full 8-st repeats) to MY, p1A&B for gusset, SMX.

Gusset section note: The single st (p1A&B), between the markers has become the final st of your round. This st is the start of your gusset. The marker directly following it, to the left, is MX. The marker to the right is MY. The area with more sts, between MX and MY, is your charted zone, where repeats of the chart (plus, Column 9 at the end to be worked after all the full 8-st repeats) will be worked as set. The number of sts in the gusset (between MY and MX) will grow as sts are increased. You will always work the gusset in garter stitch with both yarns held together. You will increase at the edges of the garter-stitch zone between MY and MX. Increases will always be worked directly after (to the left of) MY and directly before (to the right of) MX in the knit rounds of the garter-stitch gusset extending from Rounds 3, 9, 15 and 21 of Shantay V.

★★Increase Round: Work pattern as set between MX and MY, SMY, splitA&B, kA&B until 1 st remains, splitA&B in gusset, SMX. (2 sts inc) *44 (44, 44, 52, 52) sts*

Now work in pattern as set in charted zone between MX and MY, work garter stitch in Yarn A&B in gusset between MY and MX, AND AT THE SAME TIME work an Increase Round every following 6th round, 7 more times, taking increases into the garter stitch gusset. Your increase cycle should finish after working a second Row 21 of chart. (14 sts inc) *58 (58, 58, 66, 66) sts*

INCREASING CHARTED ZONE

You will now transfer 16 sts out of the 'old' garter-stitch gusset and into the charted zone. These 16 sts will allow for 2 more repeats of Shantay V to be added to the charted zone; 1 repeat at the beginning (by moving MX backwards, to the right) and 1 repeat at the end (by moving MY forwards, to the left). You will start a 'new' gusset from the single st (that was st 9 of your old gusset) between the replaced MX and MY. You will work increases into the new gusset in the same way that you did when shaping the old gusset (to make another downwards-pointing triangle). The next 5 rounds will guide you through extending the charted zone and establishing a new gusset.

Round 1 (partial): Work Row 22 of Shantay V as set between MX and MY, p9A&B of old gusset, remove MX from its current position and replace it here. Round now starts here.
Round 2 (partial): P4A&B, k1A, p3A&B to prepare for the additional repeat to be added to the beginning of extended charted zone, work Row 23 of Shantay V as set to 1 st before MY, removing MY as you go, work an extra repeat over the next 8 sts, k1A&B (instead of st in Column 9), replace MY here, k1A&B for new gusset.

Note: At the beginning of the next round, the garter stitch over the first 7 sts will be interrupted. These are the 7 sts from the end of the old gusset that now flow into the extra repeat added to the beginning of the extended charted zone. The garter stitch will be interrupted with a double purl round on the RS between where the round now starts to where MX used to be. This doubling helps the pattern flow and is almost invisible (unlike the double rounds of knit you can see on the WS).

Round 3: Work Row 24 of Shantay V between MX and MY as set, working the boxed repeat 7 (7, 7, 8, 8) times until the final st before MY, p1A&B (instead of st in Column 9 of the Shantay V), p1A&B between MY and MX for gusset.

Round 4: Work Row 1 of Shantay V between MX and MY as set, working the boxed repeat 7 (7, 7, 8, 8) times until the final st before MY, k1A&B (instead of st in Column 9 of the Shantay V), k1A&B between MY and MX for gusset.
Round 5: Work Row 2 of Shantay V between MX and MY as set, working the boxed repeat 7 (7, 7, 8, 8) times until the final st before MY, p1A&B (instead of st in Column 9 of the Shantay V), p1A&B between MY and MX for gusset.★★★

Size XS only
Repeat from ★★, stopping when you have worked 7 more pairs of increases. Your final increase should fall on a Row 15 of Shantay V. *72 (-, -, -, -) sts*

Sizes S-XL only
Repeat from ★★ to ★★★, working a total of 8 pairs of increases. *- (74, 74, 82, 82) sts*
Repeat from ★★, extending the charted zone to fit – (9, 9, 10, 10) 8-st repeats and establish a new gusset to increase in. Stop when you have worked 3 more pairs of increases in new garter stitch gusset. Your final increase should fall on a Row 15 of Shantay V. *- (80, 80, 88, 88) sts*

all sizes again.
72 (80, 80, 88, 88) sts
Work next 7 rounds straight according to Rows 16–22 of Shantay V.

Work next 2 rounds straight according to Rows 23 and 24 of Shantay V, working the st in Column 5 in the first and last repeat as the surrounding garter stitch using Yarn A&B (instead of according to the pattern as set for both rounds). This will make for a satisfying join (with no overlapping patterning sts) between the Sleeves and the Body going into the yoke.

Sizes S–XL only
Next round (partial): K1B, p3A&B.

all sizes again.

Break both yarns, leaving about a metre/yard tail to graft together or 3-needle cast-off the Underarm sts from Sleeve and Body later.

PUTTING UNDERARMS AND SLEEVE TOPS ON HOLD

Slide previous 15 sts on to stitch holder, removing MX and MY as you do — a length of smooth scrap yarn in a contrasting colour works fine. This is your Underarm, extending up from the garter stitch gusset. Leave remaining 57 (65, 65, 73, 73) charted sts live, on a spare needle or separate length of smooth waste yarn. These are your Sleeve Top sts.

Work second Sleeve exactly the same.

body.

The Body is worked straight up from the bottom edge to the Underarms in the round with a steek section so that the Marlisle can be worked on the RS throughout.

Note: Guidance is given for working a knotted steek (see overview on page 23) using 15 sts; 13 sts you cast on separately and will later unravel and knot, and a steek edge st on each side from the beginning and end of main cast-on). If you would prefer to work a different type of steek, substitute these steek instructions for your own at this point, making sure you can work the button and buttonhole bands as outlined.

Using Yarn A and the long-tail method, cast on 171 (187, 203, 219, 235) sts, then, using the yarn end attached to the ball of yarn, cast on 13 sts using the backwards loop method – these 13 sts will become part of your steek section. Join in the round being careful not to twist.
184 (200, 216, 232, 248) sts

STEEK SECTION INSTRUCTIONS

The steek section comprises 15 sts: the 13 sts created with the backwards loop cast-on and an edge st to either side from the beginning and end of the long-tail cast-on. These 13 sts should always be knitted (not purled). Work a central single st (st 7 of of these 13 sts ie st 8 of the steek section) in the most striking colour of the combo you are using (it doesn't matter if you change to the other one midway — you will be cutting it anyway) and work the 6 sts to either side holding both yarns together. This makes the steek section easy to see and the central single-colour st creates a clear guideline you can easily cut down later. These 13 sts are what will be knotted and unravelled once cut.

The first and last st of the long-tail cast-on, to either side of the 13 backwards loop cast-on sts, are the steek edge sts and should be worked in Yarn B throughout, except where Yarn B sts from the charted section would butt up against them, in which case, use Yarn A. The edge sts work as a guideline for you to make knots against and pick up and knit from for the button bands. They will not be seen on the RS of the cardigan.
169 (185, 201, 217, 233) body sts + 15 steek sts

Garter Round 1: K1B for edge st, PMX to mark start of charted zone and BOR, knit with Yarn A&B held together to end of charted zone, PMY to mark end of charted zone, k1B for edge st, k6A&B, k1B, k6A&B for steek.
Next Round (partial): K1B for edge st. Round now starts here at MX.
Garter Round 2: Purl with Yarn A&B held together to end of charted zone, SMY, k1B (edge st), k6A&B, k1B, k6A&B, k1B (edge st) for steek section, SMX.

You will work from Shantay V (V, A, V, A) chart or written instructions (see Glossary).

Set-up Round 1: Working from Set-up Row 1 of Shantay V (V, A, V, A), work 8-st repeat 21 (23, 25, 27, 29) times across the round, work Column 9, SMY, k1B (edge st), k6A&B, k1B, k6A&B, k1B (edge st) for steek section, SMX.

The previous 3 rounds set how you will work the steek section, including edge sts, throughout Body and Yoke. Instructions for how to work these 15 sts will not be given specifically in all round-by-round instructions as they are always worked as described above. The charted zone will be worked according to Shantay V (V, A, V, A) (and later Shantay Shaping V (V, A, V, A)), depending on your chosen size.

Continue as set, working from Set-up Row 2, then Rows 1-24.

Note: From now on, when working Shantay V (V, A, V, A) for the Body you will only repeat Rows 1-24, NOT Set-up Rows 1-2.

Repeat Rows 1-24 of Shantay V (V, A, V, A), a further 2 (2, 2, 2, 3) times and Rows 1-22 once only to Underarms.

Work Rows 23 and 24, working the st in Column 1 (5, 1, 5, 1) in repeat 6 (6, 7, 7, 8) and 16 (18, 19, 21, 22) as the surrounding garter stitch using Yarn A&B instead of in the pattern as set, to avoid a lone st breaking the patterning in the centre of the Underarm.

PREPARING TO PUT BODY UNDERARMS ON HOLD
169 (185, 201, 217, 233) body sts + 15 steek sts

Without knitting, ignoring the first 33 (37, 41, 45, 49) sts on your needle, thread a piece of smooth waste yarn through next 15 sts for first (right) Body Underarm and secure, but don't slip these sts off needle. Ignoring the next 73 (81, 89, 97, 105) sts, thread a piece of smooth waste yarn through next 15 sts for second (left) Body Underarm and secure, but don't slip these sts off needle.

When you start the join Body and Sleeve Tops for the Yoke, these two sets of 15 sts will be left on hold and you will have 139 (155, 171, 187, 203) sts remaining for Body (plus 15 steek section sts).

joining body and sleeve tops.

Note: When joining Body and Sleeves, make sure the Sleeve Underarms face the Body Underarms.

Next Round (dec): Working from Row 1 of Shantay V (V, A, V, A), work 8-st repeat until 1 st of Right Front remains before 15 on-hold right Body Underarm sts.

SskA&B (A, A, A, A) this final st from Right Front with first st of right Sleeve Top and slide secured right Body Underarm sts off the needle.

Continue in pattern as set across right Sleeve Top until 1 st of right Sleeve Top remains before on-hold Sleeve Underarm sts. K2togA&B (A, A, A, A) this final st from right Sleeve Top with first st of Back.

Continue in pattern as set across Back until 1 st remains before 15 on-hold left Body Underarm sts.

SskA&B (A, A, A, A) this final st from Back with first st of left Sleeve Top and slide secured left Body Underarm sts off needle.

Continue in pattern as set across left Sleeve Top until 1 st of left Sleeve Top remains before on-hold Sleeve Underarm sts. K2togA&B (A, A, A, A) this final st with first st of Left Front.

Continue in pattern as set across Left Front to 1 st before MY, work Column 9, SMY, work steek section, SMX. (4 sts dec) *249 (281, 297, 329, 345) yoke sts + 15 steek sts*

Work Rows 2-23 of Shantay V (V, A, V, A) working the boxed repeat 31 (35, 37, 41, 43) times across the round.

END OF WORKING FROM SHANTAY V AND A CHART

Pause to 3-needle cast-off the Underarms. Doing it as soon as you have enough rounds to do so will help secure them and prevent the sts distorting further. Work the cast-off with the extra length of Yarn A you left attached at the end of knitting the Sleeve. By working the cast-off with Yarn A only, this will leave you with the Yarn B end to sew together any little hole that remains at the starting end of the cast-off.

yoke shaping.

Worked on from existing live Yoke sts using Shantay Shaping V (V, A, V, A) chart, and written instructions for short rows and decs, while maintaining steek section as set.

SHANTAY SHAPING A CHART (sizes M and XL)

When using Shantay Shaping A, work the boxed repeat - (-, 37, -, 43) times across the round until 1 st remain before MY, work Column 9, SMY, work steek section, SMX.

SHANTAY SHAPING V CHART (sizes XS, S and L)

When using Shantay Shaping V, work the stitch from Column 1, then work the boxed repeat 30 (34, -, 40, -) times across the round, work Columns 10-17, SMY, work steek section, SMX.

Where you work the short rows, you will work all 3 partial rows that form the short-row cycle in the st pattern as set by the row of the chart you are working the short row on. You do not progress to the next chart row until you have finished the backwards and forwards of the short-row cycle that returns you to the BOR. Work the short rows so that the sts stacked on top maintain the stocking stitch and garter stitch on the RS in the same yarn colours/combinations. You need to work the pattern from the WS after the first w&t until you w&t again. When working the WS, you will need to work the single-yarn sts as purls so that the stocking stitch is maintained on the RS and have the floats of the other yarn facing you, so they stay hidden on the WS. Be mindful to keep your floats loose enough. You will work 10 (10, 12, 12, 12) short-row cycles as indicated in the written instructions on the rounds specified for your size.

Rounds not mentioned below are worked as per chart (with NO decs or short-rows).

Round 1 (short-row) (all sizes): Work 240 (272, 280, 312, 328) sts according to Row 1 of chart, w&t round following st, still working from Row 1, but on WS with floats on WS, work 231 (263, 263, 295, 311) sts in pattern as set, w&t round following st, work to end of round according to Row 1 as set, working wrap with the wrapped st as you pass it.

Note: On the next chart round, remember to work the remaining wrap with the wrapped st as you pass it. Do this on all future rounds after a short row round, whenever you encounter an unworked wrapped st.

Round 2 (dec) (all sizes): Work according to Row 2 of chart. (62 (70, 74, 82, 86) sts dec) *187 (211, 223, 247, 259) yoke sts + 15 steek sts*

Round 3 (short row) (all sizes): Work 171 (195, 204, 228, 240) sts according to Row 3 of chart, w&t round following st, still working from Row 3, but on WS with floats on WS, work 155 (179, 185, 209, 221) sts in pattern as set, w&t round following st, work to end of round according to Row 3 as set, working wrap with the wrapped st as you pass it.

Round 7 (short row) (all sizes): Work 165 (189, 198, 222, 234) sts according to Row 7 of chart, w&t round following st, still working from Row 7, but on WS with floats on WS, work 143 (167, 173, 197, 209) sts in pattern as set, w&t round following st, work to end of round according to Row 7 as set, working wrap with the wrapped st as you pass it.

Round 9 (short row) (all sizes): Work 162 (186, 192, 216, 228) sts according to Row 9 of chart, w&t round following st, still working from Row 9, but on WS with floats on WS, work 137 (161, 161, 185, 197) sts in pattern as set, w&t round following st, work to end of round according to Row 9 as set, working wrap with the wrapped st as you pass it.

Round 11 (short row) (all sizes): Work 159 (183, 186, 210, 222) sts according to Row 11 of chart, w&t round following st, still working from Row 11, but on WS with floats on WS, work 131 (155, 149, 173, 185) sts in pattern as set, w&t round following st, work to end of round according to Row 11 as set, working wrap with the wrapped st as you pass it.

Round 13 (short row) (all sizes): Work 156 (180, 183, 207, 219) sts according to Row 13 of chart, w&t round following st, still working from Row 13, but on WS with floats on WS, work 125 (149, 143, 167, 179) sts in pattern as set, w&t round following st, work to end of round according to Row 13 as set, working wrap with the wrapped st as you pass it.

Round 17 (short row) (sizes M, L and XL ONLY): Work – (-, 180, 204, 216) sts according to Row 17 of chart, w&t round following st, still working from Row 17, but on WS with floats on WS, work – (-, 137, 161, 173) sts in pattern as set, w&t round following st, work to end of round according to Row 17 as set, working wrap with the wrapped st as you pass it.

Round 19 (short row) (all sizes): Work 150 (174, 177, 201, 213) sts according to Row 19 of chart, w&t round following st, still working from Row 19, but on WS with floats on WS, work 113 (137, 131, 155, 167) sts in pattern as set, w&t round following st, work to end of round according to Row 19 as set, working wrap with the wrapped st as you pass it.

Round 20 (dec) (all sizes): Work according to Row 20 of chart. (62 (70, 74, 82, 86) sts dec) *125 (141, 149, 165, 173) yoke sts + 15 steek sts*

Round 21 (short row) (all sizes): Work 85 (101, 100, 116, 124) sts according to Row 21 of chart, w&t round following st, still working from Row 21, but on WS with floats on WS, work 45 (61, 51, 67, 75) sts in pattern as set, w&t round following st, work to end of round according to Row 21 as set, working wrap with the wrapped st as you pass it.

Round 23 (short row) (sizes M, L and XL ONLY): Work – (-, 98, 114, 122) sts according to Row 21 of chart, w&t round following st, still working from Row 21, but on WS with floats on WS, work – (-, 47, 63, 71) sts in pattern as set, w&t round following st, work to end of round according to Row 21 as set, working wrap with the wrapped st as you pass it.

Round 25 (short row) (all sizes): Work 80 (96, 96, 112, 120) sts according to Row 25 of chart, w&t round following st, still working from Row 25, but on WS with floats on WS, work 35 (51, 43, 59, 67) sts in pattern as set, w&t round following st, work to end of round according to Row 25 as set, working wrap with the wrapped st as you pass it.

Round 27 (short row) (all sizes): Work 78 (94, 94, 110, 118) sts according to Row 27 of chart, w&t round following st, still working from Row 27, but on WS with floats on WS, work 31 (47, 39, 55, 63) sts in pattern as set, w&t round following st, work to end of round according to Row 27 as set, working wrap with the wrapped st as you pass it.

Round 28 (dec) (all sizes): Work according to Row 28 of chart. (62 (70, 74, 82, 86) sts dec) *63 (71, 75, 83, 87) yoke sts + 15 steek sts*

Continue from Shantay Shaping V (V, A, V, A) as given to end of Round 29.

END OF WORKING FROM SHANTAY SHAPING V AND A CHART.

Note: Your neckline will look overly large at the moment, as the sts can stretch along the needle. Your cast-off will set the size of the neckline.

cast off.

Move MX 1 st backwards, to the right, to other side of edge st, so the edge st becomes the first st of your cast-off. Including both edge sts, cast off 65 (73, 77, 85, 89) sts across charted zone from edge st to edge st using both yarns. Leave only the central 13 steek sts live, as you will be undoing these anyway.

cutting the steek.

Checking the garment: Do a few doublechecks to confirm you are happy with everything. There's no going back and redoing anything once you've cut. Try it on – the fit will be similar to when you wear the cardigan buttoned up, but with a little more space and distortion from the steek section.

Cutting the steek: When you are satisfied that you're good to go, remove the needle from the 13 remaining live sts. Starting at the neckline, use a small sharp pair of scissors to cut down the single-colour guideline sts in the centre of the steek section from neckline to bottom edge to leave 6.5 sts on either side. You have now opened up the front of your cardigan and will work each front separately.

Unravelling and knotting the steek: One round at a time, starting from the neckline, unravel the 6.5 sts up to the edge st. Do not unravel the edge st. Rather than unravelling the whole steek section straight away and risking the confusion of which strands to knot together afterwards, unravel and then tie each round as you work your way down to the bottom edge. Knot Yarns A&B together using an overhand knot, fastening the knot as close to the edge st as you can without distorting it. By using the edge st as a guide, all the knots will be nice and consistently placed. Leave the strands long. Do not trim them yet!

button band.

Start from the neckline edge of the Left Front with RS facing.
★★★Using Yarn A and circular needles, pick up and knit 152 (152, 152, 152, 176) sts along the steek edge st line on the cardigan side with the charted sts, not on the knotted side where the steek sts were. You are picking up a st in each round for neatness. In the next row you will reduce down (by almost half of what you pick up and knit) to the required number of sts for the button band.

Add Yarn B. The rest of the button band will be worked in garter stitch using Yarn A&B.

Next Row: [K2tog, k1] x 5, [k2tog] until 17 sts remain, [k2tog, k1] x 5, k2tog. 71 (71, 71, 71, 83) sts dec. *81 (81, 81, 81, 93) sts*

Knit 9 rows. Cast off using Yarn A&B. The cast-off should create a 6th garter ridge on the RS.

buttonhole band.

Start from the bottom edge of the Right Front with RS facing. Work as for Button Band from ★★★ to ★★★.

Work 2 rows of garter stitch in Yarn A&B to finish at the bottom edge, then, work buttonhole rows using Yarn A&B held together throughout for 7 (7, 7, 7, 8) buttonholes:
Buttonhole cast-off row (RS):
K4, [cast off 3 sts, k9] x 6 (6, 6, 6, 7), cast off 3 sts, k2.
Buttonhole cast-on row (WS):
Knit to end casting on sts across the cast-off sts in last row using tip below.

***Buttonhole Cast-On Tip:** In final st before a cast-off section, kfb. This makes the first st of the 3 sts needed to replace those cast-off. Turn your work so the sts just worked are on the needle in your left hand, rather than the right. Cable cast-on a new st and put it on the left needle. This is the second st. Start making the third st, but before putting the new loop from the right needle on to the left needle, move the yarns forward (from back to front) between the sts (the last one knitted and the one you are just finishing), then put the new st on left needle. This puts the yarns on the correct side, so you can turn the work and start knitting.*

Knit 5 rows of garter stitch for 2 garter ridges. Cast off using Yarn A&B. The cast-off should create a 6th garter ridge and should make the Buttonhole Band equal size as the Button Band.

finishing.

Weave in all standard ends as usual. For the steek strands, get yourself some refreshment and a long needle with a sharp point and a large eye, and settle in for a good round of crafting. Catch the ends of the steek strands into the WS of the cardigan fronts – splitting the backs of sts and the floats for about 2.5cm/1". As naughty as it sounds, you actually need to insert your needle through the yarn floats and back of sts as you are skimming the ends through. You may find it easier to thread the needle before or after you have slid it into the floats at the back of the knitting. Work out what feels best for you, but try both. Trim ends, leaving about 1cm/½" poking out and being careful to not cut any of the floats from the back of the cardigan.

For easier blocking (so you can treat it as a sweater), sew up both sides of button bands using a smooth, strong thread you will pull out once dry. Give it a good soak in your favourite wool-friendly detergent. Rinse, then squeeze out excess water, wrapping in a towel to get out even more moisture. Do not wring. Block to size. Once dry, remove thread you sewed fronts closed with, then sew on buttons to correspond with top end of buttonhole and slightly closer into the body. This should ensure that the buttons sit correctly in the buttonhole, which is often not the case if you sew the button on bang in-line with the middle of the corresponding buttonhole.

DELFTIG

/dɛlftɪg/

Delftig is a play on words in Dutch, melding Delft, the name of the town where the famous blue and white ceramics come from (and where my dad used to work) and *deftig*, meaning refined. It is a word I have made up. My family loves playing with words, and it happens across all the languages spoken in our homes. Some of our joking is transferable to what others might enjoy and find funny, but much of it belongs firmly in our private microcosmos of humour, where it can easily become *melig*, as you would say in Dutch. *Melig*, used in this sense, is a word that has no parallel in English. It defines a state of hilarity that happens amongst a specific group of people who know each other very well: where you egg each other on and it gets really silly. It can only happen once you have been spending consistent time with each other, say, at the end of the night. It doesn't happen when you first walk through the door, regardless of how well you know each other or when you last were together. It involves lots of laughter, often to the point of uncontrollable giggles.

The English-speaking world has recently been introduced to *hygge*, a Danish word that does not have a properly corresponding word in English (but does have good parallels with the Dutch *gezellig*). It describes an all-round concept of cosy contentedness, which is apparently easier to attain if you have a word for it in your native language. Now that it has entered the English lexicon we can start to have access to it too, or at least understand more clearly what we have been missing out on. When a word exists for something, it allows it to be understood collectively and thereby become more frequently possible. Maybe it's time we all got to be *melig* too. My dad (who grew up in an English-speaking country) often mentions the decades after moving to London that it took him to understand British humour. This bears testimony to the fact that comprehension isn't necessarily language-based, but is also found in its local usage. Speaking a language is a huge part of being able to become part of a community, but there are more hoops to jump through before belonging, especially if you were not born with the instant access of a common tongue. Being able to play with a language and make jokes is a next step in understanding how a society works.

My parents don't sound like they were raised in the UK, or look as though their great-great-grandparents were British — and they've passed that on to me. They have now both lived in London for more than half their lives, but that doesn't stop people asking them where they come from. My father was born in New York City and my mother in Kampen (in The Netherlands). They met in the 1960s, in Amsterdam, where my mother worked. My father had been given a plane ticket by his parents to visit his new niece in the south of France (his big sister had married a Frenchman and started their family there), and afterwards he travelled to The Netherlands, where he worked as an architect in Amsterdam (and later Delft).

My parents first lived together in Amsterdam. After a few years, they decided to move elsewhere. Housing was hard to come by. Also, as the multilingual Dutch were keen to practise and show off their English, it was hard for my father to learn enough Dutch to get by on an equal footing professionally. My parents thought they would try London for a year and then move on. It was a compromise: still close to my mother's family in The Netherlands but closer language-wise to the English my father grew up with. They had many friends living there already who were originally from all sorts of other places. That year rolled into many more. I was born. Eight years later, my sister was born and all the conversations about where to move next never carried our nuclear family anywhere else.

Family holidays took us to visit Grandpa and Grandma in Manhattan, and Oma and Opa in Groene-kan, to Chabeuil, to see my aunt and her family, and Valtopina, Italy, to see my uncle and his family. (My mother's big brother had married an Italian, and moved to her tiny home village in Umbria to raise their family.) In living memory, my family have all moved of their own volition — for love, adventure, work and other practicalities — not as refugees. My grandparents' parents were either born in New York or arrived there before it became necessary for many Jews and others of their generation to flee Europe.

The majority of the friends I have and grew up with are mixes too. Generally, if my friends are British, their partners aren't. This has always been my version of normal. Passports, place and parentage aren't the be-all and end-all of belonging. It's more complicated than that. My family, friends and London are filled with people from all over, with whom I feel a shared understanding of belonging. We know it is possible to feel a special connection to the range of places that make up our heritage. In that specialness, there is also an understanding of the bitter-sweetness of having a far-flung family.

yarn pairing notes.

Ioana van Deurzen lives in The Netherlands. She's keeping the traditions of her Romanian grandparents alive with Moeke Yarn, which she runs with her brother, Radu, and his wife, Simina, who still live in Romania, where the yarn is organically raised and spun. Saskia Maas of Ovis Et Cetera is a Dutch woman, living and dyeing in Germany with her American husband. The Quadruple Dutch base she dyes on is an equal mix of four different fibres: Shetland, Merino, Blue du Maine and the non-sheepy, alpaca. The name is a wonderful play on 'double Dutch' and makes the yarn perfect for this book, even more so because none of the breeds it contains are native to The Netherlands, but they are all raised there and spun together into a beautiful yarn in neighbouring Germany. These yarns are further united by another mixed 'Dutch' woman, Saskia de Feijter (born in Belgium to Belgian and Dutch parents). She owns Ja, Wol, a yarn shop, surrounded by other independent businesses on Zwaanshals in Rotterdam, where both these yarns are stocked. I am always happy and welcomed there, through bonds of friendship and business.

When I was trying to think of a traditionally Dutch colourway that avoided the royalist orange favoured as a national identifier, blue and white immediately came to mind — from the quintessentially Dutch ceramics that have interesting links to historical trade routes with Japan and else-where. Ovis Et Cetera does have a variegated white-and-blue colourway called Delft Blauw, which was one of the inspirations for using

Saskia Maas's yarn for this pattern. However, as Moeke Yarns provides the white, a new, semi-solid blue colourway was needed. Kindly Saskia obliged, doing me the great honour of dyeing a special new colourway to go with this book. It is named Arnhemse Blauw after a rare form of Dutch blue and white pottery that originates in the city of Arnhem (where coincidentally, but unsurprisingly given the wide-ranging branches of my family, my mother spent much of her youth).

construction and fit.

Worked from the cuff up, both the pattern on the back and front of these mittens offers something new and exciting to the adventurous knitter. The front panel is intensely worked, requiring you to switch from knitting Yarn A, to purling Yarn A&B together, to knitting with Yarn B and back again in dense fabric. Satisfyingly, the tip of the mitten tapers to a point that perfectly frames the uninterrupted diamond patterning on the front. The back will be a little more familiar, but equally engaging to work. It starts with corrugated rib at the cuff to ensure a good fit, gathering the knit in, to keep the mitten on. Designed to keep out the winter weather, the palm of these mittens is thicker than the front to keep hands insulated from the thrilling chill of throwing snowballs and padded from the injustice of falling over on slippery ice. The Shadow Stripe Garter Stitch structure comprises a round of 1x1 standard stranded colourwork using each yarn singly, alternated with a round of purl using both yarns held together. It is worked in this way for the density of the fabric and stitch gauge in comparison to the front of the mitten, and for its ghostly-stripe visual effect, but also for the texture it creates on the inside, next to the sensitive palm of the hand. Plain garter stitch would be much bumpier. The afterthought thumb is the only part of the mitten that is worked differently to accommodate for right and left hand.

sizing.
S (M, L)
Designed to be worn with minimal ease.

yarn.
Yarn A: Moeke, Elena Single (4ply/fingering; 100% Romanian wool; 330m/361yds per 100g/3½oz)
Natural x 60g

Note: Be aware that skeins of Moeke yarn come in different weights, rather than a standardised 50g/1¾oz or 100g/3½oz, or set meterage/yardage per skein. Moeke is a single-ply yarn, meaning it can be worked at a wide range of gauges. It is on the heavier end of 4ply/fingering weight yarns and heavier in comparison to Yarn B. If you decide to substitute Yarn A, it is not advised to go any thicker. If you go for something a little finer, you may want to use that same weight for Yarn B (ie something a little heavier than the suggested Yarn B).

Yarn B: Ovis Et Cetera, Quadruple Dutch (lace; 25% Shetland, 25% Merino, 25% alpaca, 25% Blue du Maine; 275m/300yds per 50g/1¾oz)
Arnhemse Blauw x 1

Note: Quadruple Dutch is a 2ply laceweight (at the heavy end of laceweight) that can easily be worked to a looser gauge because of how it blooms with a slight halo from the alpaca. There's a chance, with some playing of yarn chicken, that you'll manage to get two pairs of size S and even one pair of S and one M from a single skein. In terms of substitution, a light 4ply/fingering weight could also be used, especially if Yarn A was being substituted for something finer. Or you could try a combo of two more standard 4ply/fingering weights together.

worn by...
Anna in Natural and Arnhemse Blauw, size M, knitted by Anna Maltz. The yellow dress is sewn by Marilla Walker from her Isca pattern.

needles.
3.25mm (US3) needles suitable for working small circumferences in the round.

Always use a needle size that will result in the correct gauge after blocking.

gauge.
34 stitches x 36 rounds = 10cm x 10cm/4" x 4" over Corrugated Broken Rib after blocking. (For Cuff on Palm.)
28 stitches x 42 rounds = 10cm x 10cm/4" x 4" over Shadow Stripe Garter Stitch after blocking. (For Hand on Palm.)
25 sts x 37 rounds = 10cm x 10cm/4" x 4" over Delftig Diamond stitch pattern after blocking. (For Front.)
1 Delftig Diamond pattern square of 14 sts x 14 rounds = 5cm x 3.75cm/2"x 1½" after blocking (For Front.)

Swatching note: Only one needle size will be used to achieve all 3 of these different gauges. The different gauges come from the configuration of stitches and the combination of how the yarns are used to form the different stitch structures used in the mitten. Focus on choosing a needle size that will give you the correct gauge of 25 sts x 37 rounds for the Delftig Diamond. The hope is the other 2 gauges will be achieved using this same needle size, but if they vary a little, that is OK (because you can't use a different needle size to work them anyway).

Overall, you are aiming for dense fabric to keep your hands toasty and the winter weather out. The Shadow Stripe Garter Stitch is the densest of the gauges because of the stitch structure. In order for the Shadow Stripe Garter Stitch fabric to not be too dense, the Corrugated Broken Rib and Delftig Diamond fabrics will be less dense in comparison. On its own the Delftig Diamond fabric may seem a little looser than what you might ordinarily use for a mitten, but if you make this fabric denser (with a tighter gauge), the Shadow Stripe Garter Stitch would be stiff as a board.

You can chose to knit a circular swatch (see note in The Fabric chapter, page 23) or simply start knitting a mitten, because it is almost the same size as the swatch you would work anyway. If you get gauge, continue with your mitten. If not, this was not a mitten, it was just a swatch. If it is a swatch, don't undo it until you can compare it with the other(s) to see which you prefer.

notions.
tapestry needle
2 stitch markers
smooth waste yarn in contrast colour for working afterthought thumb

glossary.
CORRUGATED BROKEN RIB
(worked in the round over a multiple of 2 sts + 1)
Round 1: K1B, [k1A, k1B] to end.
Round 2: K1B, [p1A, k1B] to end.

SHADOW STRIPE GARTER STITCH
(worked in the round over a multiple of 2 sts + 1)
Round 1: K1B, [k1A, k1B] to end.
Round 2: K1B, [pA&B] to last st, k1B.

pattern notes.

Cast-on and Corrugated Broken Ribbing: Corrugated ribbing, whether broken or regular, gives fabric a very distinct WS because of the floats. Unlike ribbing worked in a single colour (which lies flat), the colourwork gives corrugated ribbing a tendency to curl up on the RS. One of the ways to minimise this is to work your cast-on a little tight. Obviously you need to ensure it doesn't gather the sts and that you can still get your hand through the Cuff of the mitten, but err on the side of tight, rather than loose.

Adjusting for hand length, thumb placement or round gauge: If you wish to make any adjustments, calculate down from the tip of the mitten, so that the patterning stays correctly placed for the Mitten Top.

Colour dominance: To avoid colour-dominance issues, it's worth being consistent with how you hold your yarns on the Palm side of these mittens. Holding Yarn A in the position you are most comfortable purling with will make the Cuff ribbing easier to work.

Catching floats: There is no need to catch your floats, as they will make the pattern harder to work and affect the clarity of the pattern on the RS. Give them a little special attention over the longest spans, so they are neither too tight (will gather the pattern and make the mitten smaller) or too loose (will weaken the fabric and increase chance of finger-snagging inside).

schematic.

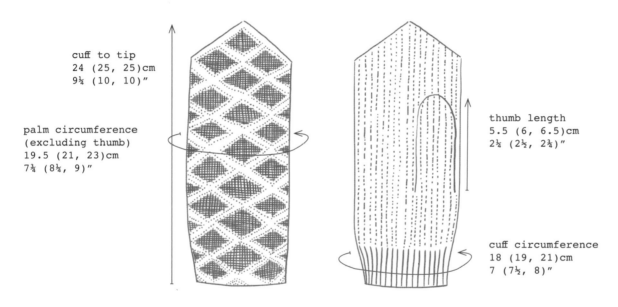

cuff to tip
24 (25, 25)cm
9¼ (10, 10)"

palm circumference
(excluding thumb)
19.5 (21, 23)cm
7¾ (8¼, 9)"

thumb length
5.5 (6, 6.5)cm
2¼ (2½, 2¾)"

cuff circumference
18 (19, 21)cm
7 (7½, 8)"

corrugated broken rib.

shadow stripe garter stitch.

key.

	Worked with Yarn A&B held together
	Worked with Yarn A, with Yarn B held at back
	Worked with Yarn B, with Yarn A held at back
	knit
•	purl
	repeat
⅄	M1L
⅄	M1R
\	ssk
/	k2tog
⋀	CDD

front size S.

Round 86: Decrease on Palm side too

Round 45: Shadow Stripe Garter Stitch Row 1 on Palm side

Round 44: Thumb Placement Round on Palm side

Round 43: Shadow Stripe Garter Stitch Row 1 on Palm side

Round 17: Start working Shadow Stripe Garter Stitch (Row 1) on Palm side

Round 16: Final round using Corrugated Broken Rib (Row 2) on Palm side

front size M.

front size L.

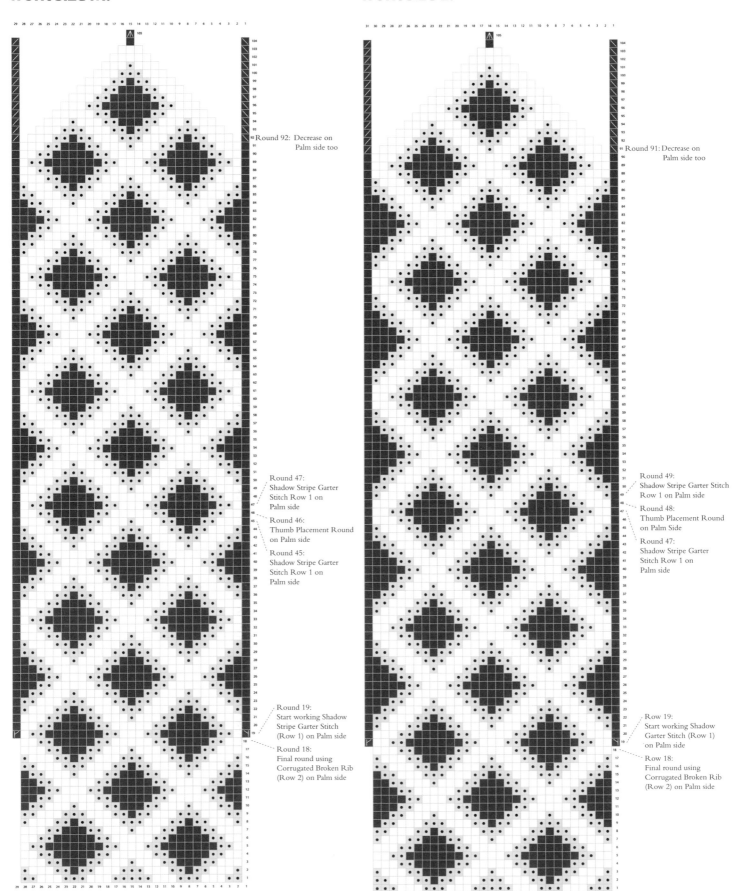

Round 92: Decrease on Palm side too

Round 91: Decrease on Palm side too

Round 47:
Shadow Stripe Garter
Stitch Row 1 on
Palm side

Round 46:
Thumb Placement Round
on Palm side

Round 45:
Shadow Stripe Garter
Stitch Row 1 on
Palm side

Round 49:
Shadow Stripe Garter Stitch
Row 1 on Palm side

Round 48:
Thumb Placement Round
on Palm Side

Round 47:
Shadow Stripe Garter
Stitch Row 1 on
Palm side

Round 19:
Start working Shadow
Stripe Garter Stitch
(Row 1) on Palm side

Round 18:
Final round using
Corrugated Broken Rib
(Row 2) on Palm side

Row 19:
Start working Shadow
Garter Stitch (Row 1)
on Palm side

Row 18:
Final round using
Corrugated Broken Rib
(Row 2) on Palm side

pattern begins.

Both mittens worked alike, except for afterthought Thumb placement.

Using Yarn A and the long-tail method, cast on 52 (56, 60) sts. Join in the round being careful not to twist. PMX to indicate BOR.

cuff.

Round 1: Work Row 1 of Delftig Front chart, PMY, work Row 1 of Corrugated Broken Rib from chart or written instructions (see Glossary) to end, SMX.

Round 2: Work Row 2 of Delftig Front chart, SMY, work Row 2 of Corrugated Broken Rib to end, SMX.

Note: MX and MY define Front and Palm sides of the mitten. The 25 (27, 29) sts from MX to MY are the Front and will be worked according to the Delftig Front chart and instructions. The Front will be increased by 2 sts (1 each side) to 27 (29, 31) sts after the Corrugated Broken Rib Cuff is completed on the Palm. The 27 (29, 31) sts from MY to MX are the Palm. They are worked according to the Palm charts (Corrugated Broken Rib for the Cuff and Shadow Stripe Garter Stitch for the Hand) and written instructions. The number of sts on the Palm will remain the same until you work decreases for the Mitten Top.

Continue as set to end of Row 16 (18, 18) of Delftig Front chart, working Corrugated Broken Rib for Cuff on Palm side of mitten throughout.

Cuff is complete. You will no longer work Corrugated Broken Rib.

hand.

Round 17 (19, 19) (inc): Work Row 17 (19, 19) of Delftig Front chart, working an M1L at the start and an M1R at the end as shown on chart, both using Yarn B, SMY, work Row 1 of Shadow Stripe Garter Stitch from chart or written instructions (see Glossary) to end, SMX. (2 sts inc) *54 (58, 62) sts*

Round 18 (20, 20): Work Row 18 (20, 20) of Delftig Front chart, SMY, work Row 2 of Shadow Stripe Garter Stitch to end, SMX.

Note: The extra Yarn-B st added at each side of the Front creates a 2-st DS between front and palm of mitten. This first and last st of both the Front AND Palm should always be a knit st using Yarn B until the Mitten Top, when the knit st is replaced by a decrease. The pattern placement does not change across the Front.

Continue as set to end of Round 43 (45, 47), working Delftig Front chart on Front and Shadow Stripe Garter Stitch on Palm.

thumb placement.

Waste yarn sts for afterthought Thumb are worked on Palm side in place of a Row 2 of Shadow Stripe Garter Stitch. These waste yarn sts will be undone later and Thumb worked on from here.

Set-up round for afterthought Thumb worked differently for right and left hand as follows:

RIGHT HAND ONLY
Round 44 (46, 48): Work Row 44 (46, 48) of Delftig Front chart, SMY, k1B, then k10 (11, 12) sts using a contrast-colour smooth waste yarn. Slide these 10 (11, 12) sts back to the left needle and knit into them alternating sts of Yarn A and B for 10 (11, 12) sts as set by Row 1 of Shadow Stripe Garter Stitch, then p15 (16, 17)A&B till 1 st remains, k1B, SMX.

LEFT HAND ONLY
Round 44 (46, 48): Work Row 44 (46, 48) of Delftig Front chart, SMY, k1B, p15 (16, 17)A&B to last 11 (12, 13) sts before MX, then k10 (11, 12) sts using a contrast-colour smooth waste yarn. Slide these 10 (11, 12) sts back to the left needle and knit into them alternating sts of Yarn A and B for 10 (11, 12) sts as set by Row 1 of Shadow Stripe Garter Stitch, k1B, SMX.

both hands again.

Round 45 (47, 49): Work Row 45 (47, 49) of Delftig Front chart, SMY, work Row 1 of Shadow Stripe Garter Stitch to end, SMX.

Continue as set to end of Round 85 (91, 90), working Delftig Front chart on Front and Shadow Stripe Garter Stitch on Palm.

mitten top.

Decrease shaping is worked each round using the first 2 and last 2 sts of both Front and Palm to decrease by 4 sts.

Round 86 (92, 91) (dec): Work Row 86 (92, 91) of Delftig Front chart, decreasing using Yarn B at beginning (sskB) and end (k2togB) as shown on chart, SMY, sskB, work in Shadow Stripe Garter Stitch in colours as set to 2 sts before end, k2togB, SMX. (4 sts dec) *50 (52, 58) sts*

Work to end of Round 96 (103, 103), working Delftig Front chart on Front and Shadow Stripe Garter Stitch on Palm with decreases as set in previous round. Break Yarn A, leaving a tail long enough to sew in later. (40 (42, 48) sts dec) *10 sts*

Round 97 (104, 104) (dec): Using Yarn B only, work Row 97 (104, 104) of Delftig Front chart, SMY, ssk, k1, k2tog on Palm, SMX. (4 sts dec) *6 sts*

Round 98 (105, 105) (dec): [CDD]B twice. (4 sts dec) *2 sts*

Pull Yarn B through 2 remaining sts and then break it, leaving a tail long enough to weave in later.

thumb.

Place 10 (11, 12) sts from above and 10 (11, 12) sts from below the waste yarn on to the needles, then carefully undo the waste yarn and pick up 1 additional st from each corner where top and bottom sts meet. *22 (24, 26) sts*

Note: The idea is to place sts, as opposed to picking up and knitting them, so that they are safely on a needle before undoing the waste yarn. In effect, the sts you place on the needle from along the bottom of the waste yarn sts (closer to the Cuff) will be regular live sts on the needle (once you have undone the waste yarn). In the first round of the Thumb, you will be able to purl into these normally, making sure to untwist them if they are on your needle backwards. The sts placed on to a needle from above (towards the Mitten Top) will be less satisfyingly 'whole' (once the waste yarn is undone) as you are working with the bottoms of sts (and with colourwork in play). The idea of having worked these sts as colourwork is that any transition kerfuffle will be made less visible by having the first round of the Thumb worked as purls with A&B held together. You may find it helps to purl into the back of them during the first round of the Thumb.

PM for BOR where the Thumb sts meet the Palm sts: with Palm facing you and Mitten Top pointing upwards, this will be on the left edge of the Thumb on the Right Mitten and on the right edge of the Thumb on the Left Mitten, towards the centre of the Palm (rather than by the DS). This way, the BOR transition and the ends to sew in will be less visible.

Round 1: Work Row 2 (purl) of Shadow Stripe Garter Stitch, working the repeat only (the repeat is boxed on the chart and in brackets in the written instructions, so you do not create a DS on each edge of the Thumb).

Round 2: Work Row 1 of Shadow Stripe Garter Stitch, working the repeat only, so that colour placement of Yarn A and B flows on from lower Palm.

Work 12 (13, 14) repeats of Shadow Stripe Garter Stitch to end with a Row 1, for approx. 5.5 (6, 6.5)cm/2¼ (2½, 2¾)" or until Thumb is just beyond desired length.

top of thumb.

Round 1 (dec): [P2togA&B] to end.
(11 (12, 13) sts dec) *11 (12, 13) sts*

Break Yarn A.

Round 2: Knit Yarn B to end.

Break Yarn B and pull yarn through remaining sts to fasten off.

Make the second mitten in same way, remembering Thumb will be placed differently on other Hand, as given in written instructions.

special finishing instructions.

Weave in all ends, using them to close any gaps and holes, especially around the Thumbs. Allow to dry flat, with the Thumbs facing upwards. Gently pull the tips into a point to exaggerate the triangular top of the mitten and make sure the DS are straight on both sides. Don't stretch out the corrugated rib at the cuff, but encourage the cast-on to lie flat.

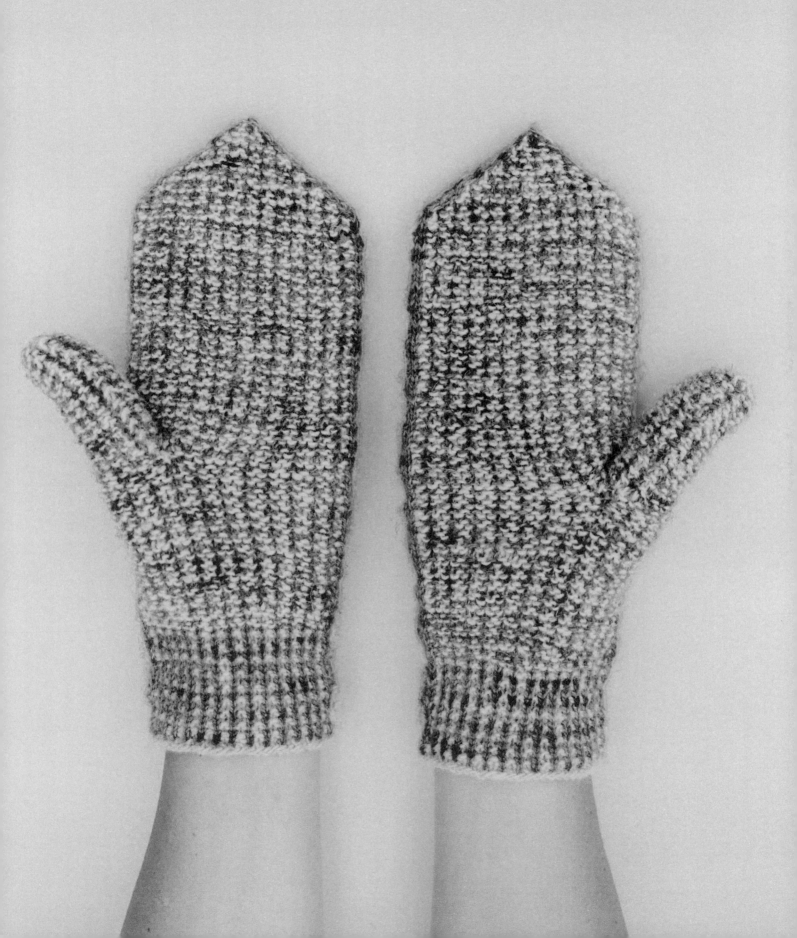

/ɛs/

ESS

The female diminutive in the English language sees names suffixed with 'ess', 'ina', 'ie' and 'y'. We are used to seeing the masculine root not as the abbreviation of the feminine, but as the source, the core. Many additions are considered a plus: home extensions, more knowledge, a welcome new member of the family, an extra zero on the pay cheque. Yet on other occasions, especially when related to women, they're seen as undesirable. When it comes to taking up extra space with their physical size, belongings, strong opinions, business acumen, sexual conquests, etc, women are subtly, if not outright, required to not have junk in the trunk.

When professional names are shared across genders, it is always the one that refers to men that takes precedence. Instead of using a neutral term, or using the extended version, any difference is hidden in the male term: seemingly to be 'fair', but ignoring the root word's long history of being a predominantly male profession. No man becomes a shepherdess, actress, waitress, or governess. It is well-documented that women still receive less income for doing the same work as men. There is a wry juxtaposition to be made in the fact that, in print, where extra characters cost extra, the feminine suffix costs more for the additional space it takes up, yet, as a woman, you are likely to get paid less for doing the job described. In the UK in 2017, Equal Pay Day, as calculated by the Fawcett Society, fell on November 10. This is the date where women, in comparison to men doing the same job, stop being paid for the work they will do for the rest of the year. It is the smartest and most easy way to illustrate the pay gap that I have encountered. A day of mourning rather than celebration.

With these thoughts in mind, this shawl, made from yarn from Daughter of a Shepherd paired with South Downs Yarn's Shepherd's Delight colourway, is called simply Ess — no root, just the bonus extra letters.

yarn pairing notes.

Daughter of a Shepherd and South Downs Yarn both have a proprietress at their helm, and both businesses were created because they each knew there was perfectly good fleece not being used. In remedying the situation, these yarns are the result.

Daughter of a Shepherd is in the capable hands of Rachel Atkinson. Rachel's dad is the shepherd on the Escrick Park Estate in Yorkshire, where the fleece from the flock of Hebrideans he tended was more expensive to shear than he would receive for the resulting fleeces from the British Wool Marketing Board. So Rachel set about turning it into yarn herself. Daughter of a Shepherd 4ply is loosely worsted spun, at John Arbon Textiles' mill in Devon, both for softness and to enhance the natural lustre and drape of the long-staple Hebridean fleece. The mill has successfully morphed the rustic fleece, often wrongly relegated to carpet wool, into a luxuriously glossy yarn with heritage.
In terms of colour, Hebridean sheep are the deepest brown, removing the need (and option) of adding any dye. It is at the lighter end of 4ply/fingering-weight yarn.

For its partner yarn, we travel the length of the colour spectrum and the country, to Sussex, where Louise Spong lives and where the creamy white Southdown sheep originates. Yet when she started looking, she couldn't find any yarn spun from this traditional local breed. Now she works with different neighbouring farmers to produce each new batch of South Downs Yarn from a specific flock. The yarn used for these shawls was spun from the Duncton flock, shepherded by David and Judy Burden. To accommodate the short staple of the Southdown fleece, it is woollen spun at the Natural Fibre Company in Cornwall. The nature of woollen-spun yarn means it blooms nicely, giving it the potential to be worked at a variety of gauges, even when, like this one, it is at the lighter end of DK/light worsted weight. Southdown sheep are white, and their fleece has a natural resistance to felting, making it a dream base for Louise's interest in dyeing with plants. Her range of pink to red shades, dyed with the likes of madder and avocado pits, is called Shepherd's Delight, yet another aspect making it the perfect complement to Daughter of a Shepherd. It all ties together so well, like raspberries and chocolate.

construction and fit.

This shawl will satisfy those who prefer to start their shawls with an epic cast-on and decrease to the finish line, rather than starting small and ending with a mammoth slog of a cast-off. In order to be able to knit it in the round (perhaps another prefered approach?) AND have the fun of some unusual construction, this shawl involves a knotted steek also found in the Ruperto Scarf (page 110) and Shantay Cardigan (page 54). Once cut, unravelled and knotted, the steek section creates the fringing. As you decrease at the edges of the steek section, your tube will taper into a funnel, so, if you are not a magic looper, make sure to change your circular needle (or DPN) length to accommodate the decreasing number of stitches.

The fabric of this shawl is designed to be reversible; it's not the same on both sides, but both are attractive and intentional.
Yarn B is worked in stocking stitch on the side you see as you work (not the RS, because it's reversible) and has its reverse stocking-stitch side obscured by the Yarn A floats on the inside (not the WS, because, again, it's reversible!). Where Yarn A&B are purled together on the side you see as you work, they make reverse stocking stitch, which shows as stocking stitch on the other side.

The small size is designed to wrap, scarf-like, around your neck, whereas the large size gives a generous shawl to envelope yourself in and keep your shoulders cosy too. Offering two sizes has the beneficial side effect of making it easy to substitute yarn weights. To be blunt, if you want to use thicker yarn, knit the smaller size on larger needles. If you want to sub for a

laceweight, use the larger size, switching your
needles out according to the effect you want.

As you can see in the photographs, there are two
options to choose from for the patterning on
your Ess Shawl: Vertically Striped or Elongated
Chequerboard. As to which one to choose, that's
up to you, but if you're a knitter who works
well with goals of the just-one-more-row or
I'll-stop-when-I-get-to-the-next-section, then
you might be happier with the checkerboard version
which has more striking carrots to work towards.
The hope is by offering two options, you might be
inspired to come up with other possibilities
using this pattern as a base. For example, you
could change the length of the bars to be longer
or shorter. Yarn colour could be changed at the
end of each chequerboard section or along the
striped version to add horizontal stripes to the
existing verticals or work in a gentle fade of
oddments. And it would certainly show off an ombre
dyed yarn very nicely. So many possibilIties...

**Consider Ess as a starting point.
The two options (and sizes)
this pattern offers for
striped and chequerboard versions
can be used as-is,
or the construction can be
borrowed to use as a blank canvas
for your own Marlisle adventure.**

sizing.

S (L)

Size S is designed to comfortably wrap around the neck, if worn scarf-style. Size L is a generous shawl that will keep your shoulders warm.

yarn.

Yarn A: Daughter of a Shepherd 4ply (4ply/fingering; 75% Hebridean, 25% Zwartbles; 400m/437yds per 100g/3½oz) Natural dark brown x 1 (2)

Yarn B: South Downs Yarn, Duncton Flock (DK/light worsted; 100% Southdown; 76m/83yds per 25g/0.9oz) Shepherd's Delight x 5 (8)

As a shawl doesn't need to fit a specific body part closely (unlike hats, mittens, socks and sweaters), you have more flexibility when substituting yarn weights. For example, you could use two same-weight yarns together or almost any combination of different weights, as long as you keep Yarn A as the finer of the two you chose, because you never use Yarn A solo. Your gauge and needle size will need to be adjusted depending on the combination you chose and the size of the shawl will be affected. If you go with finer yarns, you will want to work size L in order to have a shawl that is large enough to wrap around you. If you use heavier weight yarns, you can chose either size, depending on how big you want your shawl.

worn by...

Vonnie in Natural dark brown and Shepherd's Delight, size S using Elongated Chequerboard Option, knitted by Anna Maltz. The mint coat is sewn by Marilla Walker from her Honetone pattern, and the chambray dress from her Isca pattern.
Marilla in Natural dark brown and Shepherd's Delight in size L using Stripe Option, knitted by Emma Kylmälä. The red coat is sewn by Marilla Walker from her Honetone pattern, and the grey splatter-dyed dress from her Isca pattern.

needles.

4mm (US6) needles suitable for circular knitting.

Always use a needle size that will result in the correct gauge after blocking.

Needle type note: Because you are working this shawl in the round with a steek, starting from the longest edge and working decreases, you are in effect making a funnel. This means that, if you are not using the magic-loop method or long DPNs throughout, you will need to progressively change to a shorter length of circular needle and finally on to DPNs as your circumference decreases. Start with a 100cm/40" length.

Extra needle note: If you are inclined to tight cast-ons, it can be a good idea to cast on with a needle size one (4.5mm (US7)) or two (5mm (US8)) sizes larger. If this is the case for you, include a larger needle size to work the cast-on only. After casting on, continue with regular needle size.

gauge.

24 stitches x 32 rounds = 10cm x 10cm/4" x 4" over Ess rib stitch pattern after blocking.

However disinclined you are to make a swatch when knitting a shawl, it is a good idea for this one; to make sure you are happy with your needle size, choice of yarn and to familiarise yourself with the stitch structure before committing to the 303 or 387 sts you will cast on for the actual shawl.

As a little incentive, you can make a swatch that doubles as a fingerless mitt or wrist warmer (depending on if you decide to add a thumbhole or not). Using Yarn B and a stretchier method than the cable method you will use for the shawl, cast on 36 sts. Join in the round being careful not to twist. PM to mark BOR. Introduce Yarn A, and work rounds of [p3A&B, k3B]. For just a swatch or wrist warmer, you will need at least 12cm/5" from which to measure round gauge. If you are making a fingerless mitt, you'll want at least 15cm/6" and to pause around the 10cm/4" mark to add a thumbhole by casting off around 9 sts (in colours as set) in one round, then casting them back on again in the following round, as if making a buttonhole (you can check on the thumb instructions for the Kraai Mitts on page 34, if you want more guidance). Cast off in Yarn B only. Don't weave in the ends yet, in case it turns out you need the yarn to finish your shawl and have to frog the swatch/mitt. For the same reason, don't make a second mitt until you know you have enough yarn for your shawl.

notions.

tapestry needle
stitch marker – you may find 2 or 3 useful
small sharp scissors for cutting steek
crochet hook (for looping in extra fringing)
long-bladed fabric scissors (if you have them) to trim fringe

pattern notes.

Cast-on: A cable cast-on is advised for a number of reasons. It is neat and stable. For casting on 300+ sts it has the benefit that you work it as you go and don't need to guesstimate how long a tail to give yourself (as you do with a long-tail cast-on). If you wish to substitute a type of cast-on, make sure it is one that shows off its RS when working flat for the first row or that you accommodate for that.

Floats: Pay a little extra attention to making your floats presentable. They are part of what make the fabric reversible. Try to get into the habit of having a quick peek at your floats after every round at least. If you find one of your floats is loose some ways back, you can always twist it and knit it together with the actual st in the next round or ease out the difference across a number of sts.

Type of decrease: It's tempting to replace the slightly more arduous ssk with a quicker k2tog tbl, but it tends to create a bigger gap between the k2tog tbl and the previous stitch, forming a little ladder and a more distinct ridge of decreases.

Easing the monotony of long rounds: During the longest rounds at the start of the shawl, you may wish to put an extra marker in the middle, to help them not seem so endless and give you a target to work towards that isn't just the end of the round.

Alternating balls of yarn when there's a steek section: If working the Striped Option, unless you are entirely confident your dye lots are identical, it's worth alternating rounds of the new and old balls to avoid any difference between them affecting the overall look. If working the Elongated Chequerboard Option, you can change between balls where the Chequerboard Reversal Rounds happen, especially if this is conveniently placed to your end of ball. Or, if you are convinced your dye lots are the same (or are happy with the differences between them), you can change between balls either by spit-splicing the new and old end together (if you are in the middle of a round) or, without joining the ends in any way, place the transition of ends in the centre of the steek section. This last option will mean you don't have to join or sew in any ends at all, as you are, in effect, pre-cutting your steek for one round.

schematic.

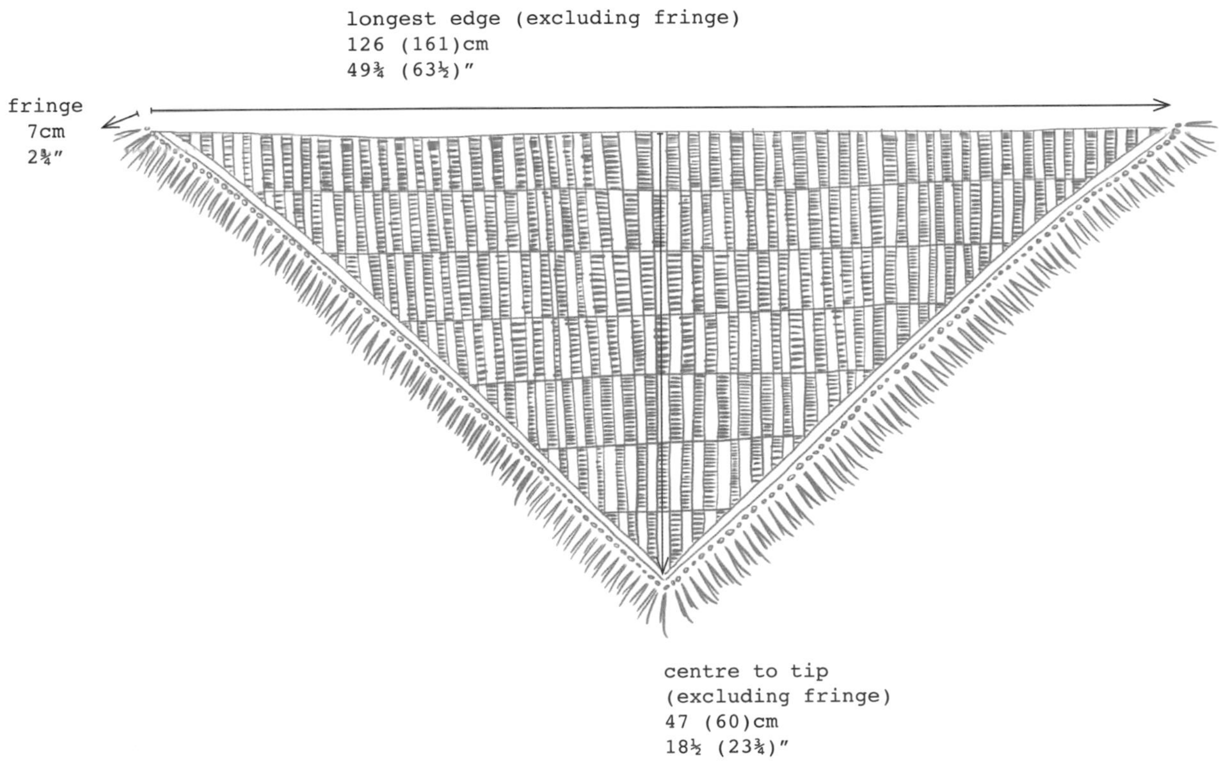

longest edge (excluding fringe)
126 (161)cm
49¾ (63½)"

fringe
7cm
2¾"

centre to tip
(excluding fringe)
47 (60)cm
18½ (23¾)"

pattern begins.

Worked in the round, with a 15-st steek section dividing the patterned shawl section. The pattern section is worked in alternating ribs of Yarn B stocking stitch and Yarn A&B reversed stocking stitch on the working side (the side you see while working – not specifically the RS, as this shawl has no right or wrong side: it is meant to be reversible). On the other side of the fabric this will show as a rib of Yarn A floats obscuring Yarn B reversed stocking stitch and a rib of Yarn A&B stocking stitch.

cast on.

Note: Because you are only casting on with Yarn B, if you are inclined to tight cast-ons, use a larger needle size to work the cast-on only. For a more extensive discussion of how to approach casting on for Marlisle in general, see page 19.

Using Yarn B and the cable method, cast on 303 (387) sts. Introduce Yarn A, leaving a 10cm/4" tail. Do not join in the round yet.

set up.

Row 1: K3B, [p3A&B, k3B] to end.

INTRODUCING THE STEEK
Cast on an additional 15 sts using both yarns held together and the backwards-loop method. Join in the round, being careful not to twist.

Note: These 15 sts are the steek section and should always be knitted (not purled) and will be worked in the same way each round until you reach the end of the shawl. Work a central single st (st 8 of the steek) in the most striking colour of the combo you are using and work the 7 sts to either side holding both yarns together. This makes the steek section easy to see and the single-colour st at the centre creates a clear guideline to cut down later. If it helps you keep track, place markers at each edge/transition of the shawl to steek section.

the shawl.

You will decrease a total of 2 sts per round, 1 st on each edge bordering the steek.

IMPORTANT NOTE: Where your Yarn A float spans more than 4 sts at the edges, as will happen with the decreases, make sure to catch it.

Round 1 (dec): K2B, sskB, p2A&B, k3B, [p3A&B, k3B] until 6 sts remain before steek section, p2A&B, k2togB, k2B, work 15-st steek section. (2 sts dec) *301 (385) shawl sts + 15 steek sts*

Regular Rib Round (dec): K2B, sskB, work in rib and yarn combos sts as set until 4 sts remain before steek section, k2togB, k2B, work 15-st steek section. (2 sts dec)

vertically striped option.

Keep repeating Regular Rib Round until 11 sts remain in the shawl (plus 15-st steek section). Finish as specified in The Tip.

elongated chequerboard option.

SECTION 1: Repeat Regular Rib Round a further 18 times. (36 sts dec) *263 (347) shawl sts + 15 steek sts*

SECTIONS 2-7 (9) ★★Rib Reversal Round: K2B, sskB, p3A&B, [k3B, p3A&B] until 4 sts remain before steek section, k2togB, k2B, work steek section. (2 sts dec)

Work Regular Rib Round 20 times. (40 sts dec) *42 sts decreased per section★★*

Note: By working a Rib Reversal Round, then repeating Regular Rib Round 20 times, you will invert the rib to start each new section and create the chequerboard. The final Regular Rib Round worked before starting each new section with a Rib Reversal Round should have, directly after the ssk (and mirrored before the k2tog at the end of the round), a p1A&B, followed by a k3B and then the rest of the ribbing, in order for the Rib Reversal Round to be placed correctly.

Now repeat from ★★ to ★★ 6 (8) more times. *11 shawl sts + 15 steek sts*

Section decrease totals: From the start of the shawl, you will decrease a total of 40 sts in Section 1: 20 sts decreased on each side. In each following section, 42 sts will be decreased in total: 21 sts decreased on each side.
Stitch counts at end of each section are as follows:
Section 1: (40 sts dec) *263 (347) shawl sts + 15 steek sts*
Section 2: (42 sts dec) *221 (305) shawl sts + 15 steek sts*
Section 3: (42 sts dec) *179 (263) shawl sts + 15 steek sts*
Section 4: (42 sts dec) *137 (221) shawl sts + 15 steek sts*
Section 5: (42 sts dec) *95 (179) shawl sts + 15 steek sts*
Section 6: (42 sts dec) *53 (137) shawl sts + 15 steek sts*
Section 7: (42 sts dec) *11 (95) shawl sts + 15 steek sts*

Size L ONLY
Section 8: (42 sts dec) *53 shawl sts + 15 steek sts*
Section 9: (42 sts dec) *11 shawl sts + 15 steek sts*

both options again.

the tip.

When 11 sts remain in shawl, break Yarn A in centre of steek section and finish as follows, working steek section in Yarn B only.

Round 1 (dec): K2, ssk, k3, k2tog, k2, work 15-st steek section. (2 sts dec) *9 shawl sts + 15 steek sts*
Round 2 (dec): K2, ssk, k1, k2tog, k2, work 15-st steek section. (2 sts dec) *7 shawl sts + 15 steek sts*
Round 3 (dec): K2, sk2po, k2, work 15-st steek section. (2 sts dec) *5 shawl sts + 15 steek sts*
Round 4 (dec): K1, sk2po, k1, work 15-st steek section. (2 sts dec) *3 shawl sts + 15 steek sts*
Round 5 (dec): Sk2po. Break yarn and pull through single remaining shawl stitch. Do not cast off the 15 steek sts.

Ess

special finishing instructions.

Cutting the steek: Remove the needle from the 15 remaining live sts. Using small, sharp scissors, cut down the centre of the 15 steek sts, along your single-colour st guideline to leave 7.5 sts on either side, from the live sts and through the backwards-loop cast-on. This will transform your shawl from a funnel to a triangle. Now is the time to imagine your shawl is a butterfly unfurling from a cocoon and opening up her wings.

Unravelling and knotting the steek: Starting at the tip of the shawl, 2 rounds at a time, unravel the 7.5 sts in both colours used and tie a basic overhand knot with the 4 ends (2 of each colour) and push snugly into the edge of the shawl. If you would like all your tassels to contain both colours, loop in extra strands of Yarn A at the start (the longest edge, by the cast-on) and tip of the shawl, where you were only using Yarn B to knit with. To do this, cut a 20cm/8" strand from your leftover Yarn A and, with the help of a crochet hook, pull through the space between the rows so that half sticks out each side. Tie it into the knot with the strands of Yarn B from the steek. As you work along the edge, make sure the knots are pushed snugly into the shawl edge, but not so tight that they distort it. By using the edge as a guide, all the knots will be nice and consistently placed. Rather than unravelling everything straight away and risking confusion of which strands to knot together afterwards, only unravel the ends you will tie together in the next knot.

Blocking the shawl: When all knots are tied, give the shawl a good soak in your favourite wool-friendly detergent. Leave it to soak for a good half an hour or more to allow the kinks in the fringing to relax and the stitches to ease into place. Rinse, then squeeze out excess water, wrapping in a towel to get out even more moisture. Do not wring. Block to size, allowing to dry flat, pinned out using blocking wires (if you have them) to minimise the amount of pins you need to use to avoid scalloped edges. With a wide-toothed comb or a fork, comb out the fringing while it's damp, to allow it to dry flat.

Trimming the fringe: Once dry, comb the fringing again. Before unpinning (so that the shawl is supported and stable), trim fringing a little to even out the edges, but don't get carried away snipping. This should leave you with at least a 7cm/2¾" fringe. Leave it as long as you can. Using fabric scissors with long blades helps keep things straight and resist additional fidget snipping.

MIDSTREAM

/mɪdˈstriːm/

Apparently you can divide those who sexually objectify/desire women's bodies into those who like tits and those who like arse. Why the need to choose, to divide? Why not like the lot (and everything above, below and in between)? It's a loaded question, in that there has been a distinct bias to focus on what's upfront and leave the behind to special-interest groups. In that sense, knits are the tits of the textile world and purls are the bottom. Whether a thrower or a picker, many knitters have an anti-purling bias. If we look at knitting as an intricate relationship between two stitches — knit and purl — it's distinctly limiting to dislike half of the principal players. You're setting yourself up to work grudgingly through a vast amount of stitches that you could have the pleasure shaping in your knitting lifetime.

I have long pondered the reasons for a common distaste for working purl stitches. There are some compelling arguments that show it is slightly more arduous to form a purl stitch, but I firmly believe that we shun purl largely because of our lack of familiarity compounded by a language-based bias. For starters, we call the whole thing we do with needles and yarn 'knitting', not 'purling'. Where's the positive role model for purls? I have never encountered a knitter who learned how to purl first. That simple fact explains why knitting, not purling, will feel more familiar to your fingers. But need it be set in stone that this remains true for ever after? Need purling always come second? It is the underdog, second-fiddle, which are reasons enough to love it. It completes, supports and furthers what is impossible in knit alone. Where would knitting be without purl?

When it comes to stitches, as in most other things, I am equal-opportunity.

I wonder if we could change things by raising a generation of knitters by teaching them to purl first. Purlers? In the same way that most of us stick with the very first cast-on method taught to us by family members, neighbours, friends, a knitting manual, the internet, etc. We branch out only when there is a good enough argument to try something else, to coax us out of our comfort zone, away from the habitual, the muscle memory in our hands, succumbing to a bit of a human inclination to pick sides. But as we all move instead to being more inclusive, can we not open our minds and fingers to purling so that one isn't prefered over the other?

After this pattern intro's crass comparison of knits and tits and the talk of objectifying female bodies, prejudice and avenues of change for old habits, I would like to dedicate this pattern to two of the great men in my life: my father, Bob, and my husband, Adam. Examples of lifelong good guys at this watershed moment when hopefully many more men will grow up to be like them, rather than like other examples of manhood that have been allowed to do damage for so long. These two yarns are paired to reflect where they come from. My father hails from New York on the East Coast of the USA and my husband from California on the West Coast. It may be the same country, but these places are geographically farther apart than New York and London, where we are all based now. With an ocean between them and their homeland, Midstream seemed an apt name for being, well, in the middle of things. The inspiration for this sweater comes from the fisherman's smock, which has long been a favourite garment among artists. Both these central male characters in my life are creatives. Being an architect from the days of hand drawing, my dad can draw a mean straight line without a ruler in sight, and I love how Marlisle allows the

stripes to appear vertically on this sweater, where they would usually only be possible horizontally. There's also a tenuous link to sailing. Bob was a merchant marine for a couple of summers when he was seventeen, working for nine weeks on a Victory Ship freighter with a crew of 48 travelling from New York to Hawaii along the Panama Canal. The following year he worked for five weeks on a ship travelling from New York to Newfoundland and back. Adam's parents had a small boat for a time when he was growing up in Torrance, California. The combination of colours were chosen to bring out the connection to water, with the bluey shades and the white crests of waves.

yarn pairing notes.

Flock is a 4ply/fingering-weight single from the West Coast of the USA. The natural white of the California Targhee and the pale grey of the Montana Rambouillet fleeces are spun together as if space-dyed, giving Midstream a subtle, striated effect. This natural shade puffs up nicely once washed, something that dyed shades will have already done while in the dye kettles. It feels a little strange to use this yarn as a natural colour, because it comes from A Verb For Keeping Warm (AVFKW or simply, Verb) which specialises in adding colour through natural dyeing. Located on San Pablo Avenue in Oakland, California, it's a dye kitchen, garden, classroom, shop and the focus of an incredible community of conscientious makers. An ark with Kristine Vejar and her partner, Adrienne Rodriguez, at the helm. I wish it had been there while I was living in the California Bay Area for five years, but I'm happy to know it is there now and that I can visit when I'm in town. To bind it even more perfectly to this project, Verb stands a few doors down from where Adam had an art gallery and project space when we first met, before we moved to London together.

The squooshy, 2ply, woollen-spun Mohonk helps tame the bias twist that is the nature of a single-ply yarn such as Flock. Mohonk is a sport-weight yarn that, like my father, hails from New York. Whereas he was born in the Bronx, the unregistered Cormo flock that produce the fleece for this yarn are raised in upstate New York, where Jill Draper dyes. The fleece is spun for her at Green Mountain Spinnery before she adds additional colours to it. I feel as though Jill is one of the instigators of Marlisle. A few years ago, we had a fleeting conversation about the ins and outs of machine knitting in comparison to hand knitting, and specifically about plating, and the apparent impossibility of achieving a similar effect by hand. A plater is a small piece of kit you can slot into the carriage of a knitting machine, which allows two different yarns to be fed through in such a way that one of them shows only on the front and the other on the back of the stitch. Worked with two different-coloured threads, this means that a single set of stitches can appear as one colour on one side and another on the reverse, making a fabric that is a different colour on each side. We had marvelled at how slow, if not impossible, that would be to replicate by hand — and in the whirring cogs of that conversation were the sparks that helped Marlisle ignite and catch fire. There are distinct overlaps between some of the effects that can be achieved with Marlisle, and those created by using the plater on a knitting machine. Since adding some knowledge of machine knitting to my arsenal of knitting skills, I like to think about how the two sympatico approaches can inform each other. In the eight years since I started machine knitting, I like to make sure that what I knit isn't better suited to the other method: so miles and miles of stocking stitch I will leave to the knitting machine, and intricate one-piece shaping in the round with changes of texture and colour — that's what hand knitting is for.

construction and fit.

Midstream is designed to be a loose comfy sweater reminiscent of a traditional fisherman's smock (as adopted by artists and other bohemians). Though it is pictured here with a straight body, you'll find guidance to tailor it to your personal body fit tastes in the Pattern Notes. Because it is knitted from the bottom up, in the round, you have the easy option to make the funnel neck longer or shorter, depending on your preference (which might be dictated by the length of your neck and/or how much yarn you have left over).

An occasional single-coloured vertical stripe in a sweater usually involves intarsia or a sideways knit (to avoid epically long floats). Marlisle allows for the decorative stripes up the front of this sweater to work. In fact, you could just work a single stripe to echo those on the back and under the arms, if you fancied it more minimal. The Marlisle stripes down the sides make a feature of what appear to be the 'seams' of the garment (even though it is knitted in the round) and create an easy reference point when counting rounds, like a built-in stitch marker. They have the added bonus of masking the jog that happens when you work garter stitch in the round, as you will for the cuffs, bottom edging and funnel neck.

The pattern is quick to memorise and very visually guided, creating a straight body and full-length sleeves with regular increases. Once the pattern is set on the body and sleeves, you can work on for a good distance without needing to check the pattern. If you have already embraced purling, this sweater is both comforting to knit and to wear. If you are purl-curious and have been wanting to try a committed purl-on-purl project, this will help you explore that side of

your knitting self and will hopefully lead to many, more pleasurable, future knitting AND purling experiences. If you really are a purl-hater, yet are still drawn to this sweater, you could, with a little smarts, adapt the pattern to work the instructions inside out.

The yoke is a raglan in the sense that the shaping is concentrated over the shoulders, rather than equally distributed around the whole circumference of the yoke. This allows the decorative stripes to travel up the front of the sweater, intact from start to finish (and the single stripe up the back remains for visual interest and to break up the monotony of long rounds). Do give yourself a little bit of quiet time to get a handle on how the first few decreases and short rows work. They have a distinct rhythm to them that will soon become apparent. (So please don't be put off by how wordy it looks when you read ahead without stitches on your needles. Just try to trust it won't be daunting when you are actually doing it.)

Feeling the same love for working purls as you do for knits doubles the pleasure.

sizing.

XS (S, M, L, XL, XXL)
Designed to be worn with 15cm/6" positive ease around bust.
It is designed to be a little oversized, so if you are on the fence
about which size to make, opt for the smaller of the two so it
doesn't get too roomy.

yarn.

Yarn A: A Verb For Keeping Warm, Flock 2nd Edition
(4ply/fingering; 100% wool (blend of California Targhee and
Montana Rambouillet); 265m/290yds per 50g/1¾oz)
Granite (natural) x 4 (4, 5, 5, 6, 6)

Yarn B: Jill Draper Makes Stuff, Mohonk (sport; 100% New York
State unregistered Cormo wool; 338m/370yds per 113g/4oz)
Pale Lapis or Dark Wash Denim x 4 (4, 5, 5, 6, 6)

*Yarn B note: The actual weight of skeins of Mohonk tend to be
generous. The specified amount of skeins required to make a Midstream
Sweater is based on them weighing 113g/4oz. For a more extensive
discussion on this topic, see Quantity on page 10.*

worn by...

Adam in Granite and Pale Lapis, size M, knitted by Anna Maltz.
Anna in Granite and Dark Wash Denim, size M, knitted by
Anna Maltz.

gauge.

19 stitches x 27 rounds = 10cm x 10cm/4" x 4" over reverse
stocking stitch using both yarns held together on larger needle
size after blocking. (Main gauge.)

19 stitches x 38 rounds = 10cm x 10cm/4" x 4" over garter stitch
using both yarns held together on smaller needle size after
blocking. (For Cuffs, Bottom Edge and Funnel Neck.)

*Swatching note: To save on the 'hassle' of making a separate circular
swatch, you can start following the instructions for a Sleeve from the
beginning. Once you have about 15cm/6", leave your sts live (either by
leaving them on the needle or sliding them on to smooth cotton, linen or
a scoubidou), give it a good soak, squeeze it out all the excess water you
can, block it, let it dry, then measure your gauge on there. If it's to your
liking, just continue on with your Sleeve. If not, it wasn't destined to be
a Sleeve, it was meant to be a swatch. Retry with an adjusted needle
size. Don't unravel your first attempt until you can see your options
side-by-side.*

needles.

4mm (US6) circular needle for Bottom Edging, at least
80cm/32" long. If making sizes L, XL or XXL, your sts may fit
more easily on a 100cm/40" needle.
4mm (US6) needles suitable for working small circumferences
in the round for Cuff.
4mm (US6) 40cm/16" circular needle for Funnel Neck.
4.5mm (US7) circular needle for Body and Yoke, at least
80cm/32" long. If making sizes L, XL or XXL, your sts may fit
more easily on a 100cm/40" needle.
4.5mm (US7) needles suitable for working small circumferences
in the round for Sleeves.

Always use a needle size that will result in the correct gauge after
blocking.

*Needle type note: You need needles that will work for the small
circumference of sts in the sleeves (for example, magic loop or a combo
of DPNs and 40cm/16" circulars).*

*Extra needle note: If you will use Underarm Joining Option 1, it calls
for a 3-needle cast-off. This should be worked with a 5mm (US8) needle,
so include that in your ingredients list. This additional needle size is also
useful if you are inclined to tight cast-ons and cast-offs, as you will be able
to use it to work those too.*

notions.

tapestry needle
4 stitch markers
smooth waste yarn or stitch holder for putting Underarm sts
on hold

glossary.

FRONT DECORATIVE STRIPES (FDS)
(worked in the round over multiple of 5 sts + 3)
Every round: [K3B, p2A&B] x 4 (4, 4, 6, 6, 6), k3B] over
23 (23, 23, 33, 33, 33) sts

*Note: The FDS is always worked with p2A&B valleys (reverse stocking
stitch) between the k3B ridges (stocking stitch), regardless of whether the
surrounding marl is worked as garter stitch for the Bottom Edging and
Funnel Neck. Whether the valleys are worked in reverse stocking stitch
or garter stitch, they will create a slightly scooped edge that is a feature
of the design.*

splitA&B
Using Yarn A&B held together, knit into the Yarn A and Yarn
B sections of next stitch individually, as if they were 2 separate
stitches. 1-st increase.

schematic.

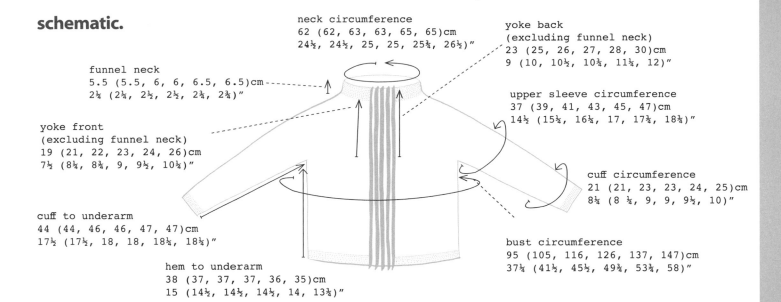

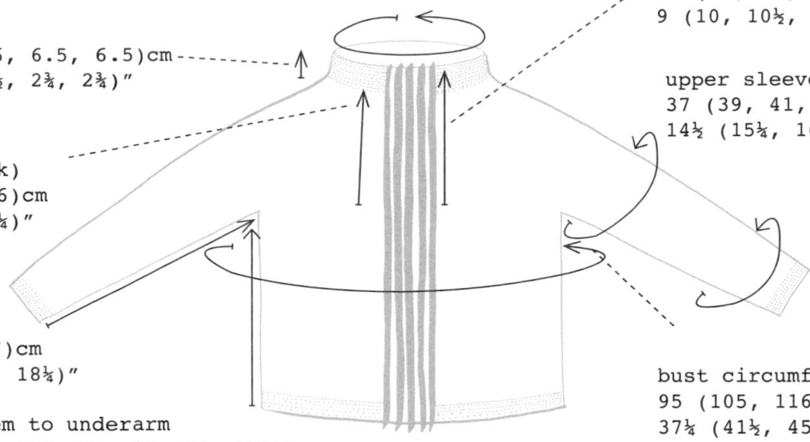
neck circumference
62 (62, 63, 63, 65, 65)cm
24½, 24½, 25, 25, 25¾, 26½)"
yoke back
(excluding funnel neck)
23 (25, 26, 27, 28, 30)cm
9 (10, 10½, 10¾, 11¼, 12)"
funnel neck
5.5 (5.5, 6, 6, 6.5, 6.5)cm
2¼ (2¼, 2½, 2½, 2¾, 2¾)"
upper sleeve circumference
37 (39, 41, 43, 45, 47)cm
14½ (15¼, 16¼, 17, 17¾, 18¾)"
yoke front
(excluding funnel neck)
19 (21, 22, 23, 24, 26)cm
7½ (8¼, 8¾, 9, 9½, 10¼)"
cuff circumference
21 (21, 23, 23, 24, 25)cm
8¼ (8 ¼, 9, 9, 9½, 10)"
cuff to underarm
44 (44, 46, 46, 47, 47)cm
17½ (17½, 18, 18, 18¾, 18¾)"
bust circumference
95 (105, 116, 126, 137, 147)cm
37¼ (41½, 45½, 49¾, 53¾, 58)"
hem to underarm
38 (37, 37, 37, 36, 35)cm
15 (14½, 14½, 14½, 14, 13¾)"

adapting midstream.

We all have wonderfully different body shapes. This sweater is designed to be roomy and cosy, not figure-hugging. The natural stretch of reverse stocking stitch will go a long way to give the garment good shaping around your body. Depending on how you like your sweaters to fit, the straight Body might not suit your own preference or the Sleeve length might need adjusting. There are all sorts of tricks to tailoring a pattern to have it fit in the way you love, beyond simply making it a few rounds shorter or longer. Here are some pointers for how you may wish to personalise the Body and Sleeves for different body shapes. The rest is up to you.

BODY

Distinct Waist: If your waist is significantly smaller than your bust and bum, you may wish to add hourglass shaping by decreasing gently around the circumference of where your natural waist is (working the DSs and FDS as they are) and then increasing back out by the same number of stitches to make sure you go into the Yoke with the correct number. Start with the single size that best fits your boobs and bum. Work out where the Body starts by measuring where the top of arm circumference will put the sweater's Underarm (this will be lower than where your actual armpit is). From here you can look at the body length measurement and decide where your natural waist falls in relation to that.

Prominent Boobs: If your boobs are the biggest part of you, consider adding short rows across the front only towards the very top of the Body to give your breasts the space they deserve without the rest of the sweater fitting you like a tent (because you've picked a bigger size to accommodate your boobs) or fitting tight across the breasts and riding up at the front because you've picked a size with not enough space for your tatas. If you intend to do this, pick a size based on your hip circumference (as if it were your bust circumference), as you will be accommodating your breasts by giving them their own special space.

Nice Pear: If the widest part of you is below your waist, consider making the Body A-line. Choose a Yoke and Sleeve size based on your bust measurement and combine it with a Body size that will fit your bum. Gently taper the the Body from the larger size around your bottom to the number of sts you need to go into the smaller sized Yoke. Decrease on both sides of the Left and Right DS: sspA&B before each side DS and p2togA&B after.

SLEEVES

The Sleeves are designed to be full length. Working from the Cuff up, the paired increases on the inside arm will bring you to 10 (15, 16, 25, 23, 19) straight Sleeve Rounds to work before the Sleeve is complete. Adjusting the number of rounds in this straight section is the easiest way to give more/less length to suit your personal preference or to accommodate for your round gauge.

For longer Sleeves (or to adjust for shorter round gauge): If you work too many more straight rounds, the top of your Sleeves will start to look bulky, especially in sizes L, XL and XXL (where there are already a good amount of straight rounds). To avoid this, work your extra rounds in the Cuff and straight section directly after the Cuff to avoid needing to fiddle with the rate of increase in the Sleeve. If you need significantly more rounds in the Sleeves, you can work 6 (5, 5, 4, 4, 4) Sleeve Rounds between Sleeve Increase Rounds, instead of the specified 5 (4, 4, 3, 3, 3) or tinker with the frequency, so it is not the same throughout. You will likely need to adjust the number of straight rounds, if you adjust the frequency.

For shorter Sleeves (or to accommodate for a longer round gauge): Make sure to leave at least 6 rounds in the straight section at the top of the Sleeves to maintain the ease of getting in and out of your sweater. If you need significantly fewer rounds in the Sleeves, you can work 4 (3, 3, 2, 2, 2) Sleeve Rounds between Sleeve Increase Rounds, instead of the specified 5 (4, 4, 3, 3, 3) or tinker with the frequency, so it is not the same throughout. This is likely to be particularly useful for sizes XS, S and M. You may need to adjust the number of straight rounds, if you adjust the frequency.

pattern begins.

sleeves.

Both Sleeves are worked alike, from the cuff up, in the round with a central DS that will run under the arm from Cuff to Underarm.

Using larger needles, Yarn B and the long-tail method cast on 40 (40, 44, 44, 46, 48) sts. Join in the round being careful not to twist. PM to mark BOR.

cuff.

Worked in garter stitch with central DS.

Change to smaller needles.

Round 1 (Cuff Round): K3B for DS, kA&B to end.
Round 2 (Sleeve Round): K3B for DS, pA&B to end.

Repeat Rounds 1-2 for garter stitch with DS until you've worked a total of 16 (16, 18, 18, 20, 20) rounds.

Change to larger needles.

main sleeve.

Worked in reversed stocking stitch with central DS.

Work 8 Sleeve Rounds.

**Sleeve Increase Round: K3B for DS, splitA&B, pA&B to end, splitA&B. (2 sts inc)

Work 5 (4, 4, 3, 3, 3) Sleeve Rounds straight.**

Repeat from ** to ** 14 (16, 16, 18, 19, 20) more times for a total of 15 (17, 17, 19, 20, 21) pairs of incs.
(30 (34, 34, 38, 40, 42) sts inc) *70 (74, 78, 82, 86, 90) sts*

Work straight for 10 (15, 16, 25, 23, 19) Sleeve Rounds.

put underarms and sleeve tops on hold.

Now it's time for a little choice. Option 1 is more aesthetically pleasing and satisfying to work, in a knitterly way, but is a bit of a fiddle. It will later involve a decision between 3-needle cast-off or grafting. Option 2 sees you simply cast off: easy, but lacks finesse. Take your pick.

OPTION 1: Underarm sts on hold
Next Round: K3B for DS, k60 (64, 67, 71, 74, 78)A&B until 7 (7, 8, 8, 9, 9) sts remain before the DS/end of round. Break yarns leaving a metre/yard tail of Yarn B (to use for the 3-needle cast-off later) and a 15cm/6" tail of Yarn A (to seal any holes while weaving in later). Slide next 17 (17, 19, 19, 21, 21) sts, with DS centrally placed, on to a stitch holder or length of smooth waste yarn for the Underarm.
53 (57, 59, 63, 65, 69) sts and 17 (17, 19, 19, 21, 21) sts on hold

OPTION 2: Underarm sts cast-off.
Next Round: K3B for DS, k60 (64, 67, 71, 74, 78)A&B until 7 (7, 8, 8, 9, 9) sts remain before the DS/end of round, then cast off 17 (17, 19, 19, 21, 21) sts, with DS centrally placed. Break yarns leaving a tail of 60cm/24": long enough to sew the Underarm closed later. *53 (57, 59, 63, 65, 69) sts*

both options again.

If you have a spare needle to work the second sleeve in the same fashion, leave Sleeve Top sts live on it, otherwise slide them on to a separate piece of smooth waste yarn and put aside while you work second Sleeve and Body. Work second Sleeve exactly the same, putting aside with first Sleeve while you work the Body.

body.

Using larger needles, Yarn B and the long-tail method, cast on 180 (200, 220, 240, 260, 280) sts. Join in the round being careful not to twist. PM to mark BOR.

Change to smaller needles.

Pattern Set-up Round:
Introduce Yarn A.
Front 90 (100, 110, 120, 130, 140) sts: K3B for Left Side DS, k32 (37, 42, 42, 47, 52)A&B, FDS, k32 (37, 42, 42, 47, 52)A&B.
Back 90 (100, 110, 120, 130, 140) sts:
[K3B for DS, k42 (47, 52, 57, 62, 67)A&B] twice.

Note: The first k3B of the Back is the Right Side DS. As you work the repeat, the second DS is the Centre Back DS.

bottom edging.

Worked in garter stitch with DSs and FDS. The Centre Back DS and FDS will run up into the Yoke. The Left/Right Side DS will be worked up to the Underarms and will line up with Sleeve DSs when the Underarms are sealed.

Round 1 (Body Round):
Front 90 (100, 110, 120, 130, 140) sts: K3B for Left Side DS, p32 (37, 42, 42, 47, 52)A&B, FDS, p32 (37, 42, 42, 47, 52)A&B.
Back 90 (100, 110, 120, 130, 140) sts: [K3B for DS, p42 (47, 52, 57, 62, 67)A&B] x 2.

Round 2 (Edge Round):
Front 90 (100, 110, 120, 130, 140) sts: K3B, k32 (37, 42, 42, 47, 52)A&B, FDS, k32 (37, 42, 42, 47, 52)A&B.
Back 90 (100, 110, 120, 130, 140) sts:
[K3B, k42 (47, 52, 57, 62, 67)A&B] x 2.

Repeat Rounds 1-2 for garter-stitch edging with FDS and DSs until you've worked a total of 14 (14, 16, 16, 18, 18) rounds.

Change to larger needles.

main body.

Worked in reversed stocking stitch maintaining DSs and FDS as set. Work 93 (93, 95, 95, 97, 97) Body Rounds straight or until work measures 38 (37, 37, 37, 36, 35)cm/15 (14½, 14½, 14½, 14, 13¾)" from cast-on edge, remembering that the specified lengths are based on the blocked measurements.

Work next round based on the option you chose for the Sleeves.

OPTION 1: Underarm sts on hold
Next Round: K3B for DS, work as set to 7 (7, 8, 8, 9, 9) sts after the Right Side DS. Slide the 17 (17, 19, 19, 21, 21) sts you just worked on to a length of smooth waste yarn with the Right Side DS centrally placed. Work across Back to 7 (7, 8, 8, 9, 9) sts before the Left Side DS/end of round. Slide next 17 (17, 19, 19, 21, 21) sts with the Left Side DS centrally placed, on to a stitch holder or length of smooth waste yarn for the Underarm.

OPTION 2: Underarm sts cast-off
Next Round: K3B for DS, work as set to 7 (7, 8, 8, 9, 9) sts before the Right Side DS. Cast off the next 17 (17, 19, 19, 21, 21) sts with the Right Side DS centrally placed. Work across Back to 7 (7, 8, 8, 9, 9) sts before the Left Side DS/end of round. Cast off next 17 (17, 19, 19, 21, 21) sts, with the Left Side DS centrally placed.

both options again.

You should have 73 (83, 91, 101, 109, 119) sts for the Front and the same again for the Back. Body is complete. Do not break yarns, you will use them to work the Yoke.

yoke.

Worked in reverse stocking stitch in Yarn A&B, maintaining the FDS and Centre Back DS in Yarn A.

JOINING BODY AND SLEEVES

Note: When joining Body and Sleeves, make sure the Underarms face each other on the Body and the Sleeves. The DS on Body and Sleeve will line up in the centre of the Underarm when they are joined.

Starting with the yarn you left live on the Body, work across 53 (57, 59, 63, 65, 69) Sleeve Top sts, then 73 (83, 91, 101, 109, 119) Front sts, maintaining the FDS, then 53 (57, 59, 63, 65, 69) second Sleeve Top sts and then across the 73 (83, 91, 101, 109, 119) Back sts maintaining the Centre Back DS. Join in the round. PM to mark new BOR. *252 (280, 300, 328, 348, 376) sts*

Work 6 (9, 8, 11, 11, 12) rounds straight.

Marker Placement Round:
Purl A&B to FDS, PMZ, FDS, PMW, pA&B to 10 (10, 10, 15, 15, 15) sts before Centre Back DS, PMX, p10 (10, 10, 15, 15, 15) A&B, k3B for Centre Back DS, p10 (10, 10, 15, 15, 15)A&B, PMY, purl A&B to end.

Next Round (partial): Work to MW, maintaining FDS. MW marks new BOR. Round now starts here for remainder of Yoke.

joining underarms.

Joining the Underarms now, as soon as you have enough fabric, helps prevent the sts at the edges from becoming further distorted by the weight of the garment and the action of knitting pulling on them.

Join the Underarms based on the same option you chose for the Body using the Yarn B tail you left for yourself. Leave the Yarn A tail at the starting edge and when you are done with the Yarn B seam, use Yarn A to close the hole that inevitably remains at the starting end of the seam. (You will have Yarn B to seal the hole at the other edge of the Underarm.)

OPTION 1: Underarm stitches on hold

Slip held sts from Body and Sleeve on to each their own DPN or ends of a similar-sized circular needle, so that needle tips face the edge where you have the yarn ends ready to work with. Choose from the following:

To work a 3-needle cast-off: Using the needle reserved for the 3-needle cast-off and the Yarn B tail. With RS facing and WS of Sleeve and Body together, knit to cast off 7 (7, 8, 8, 9, 9) sts. Flip yarn and needles to the WS and with RS of Sleeve and Body together knit to cast off the 3 DS sts. Flip yarn and needles back to the RS with WS of Sleeve and Body together and knit to cast off the remaining 7 (7, 8, 8, 9, 9) sts.

To graft (Kitchener stitch): Using a tapestry needle and Yarn B. With RS facing, graft 7 (7, 8, 8, 9, 9) sts for purl. Graft the 3 DS sts as knit, then the remaining 7 (7, 8, 8, 9, 9) sts as purl.

OPTION 2: Underarm sts cast-off

Using a tapestry needle, Yarn B and mattress stitch, sew the Underarms closed.

both options again.

yoke decreases.

Decreases are worked in the Shoulder areas, between MW to MX (Right Shoulder) and MY to MZ (Left Shoulder), not across the Front (MX to MY which exactly frame the FDS) and Back (MZ to MW with Centre Back DS). This means the FDS and Centre Back DS can run smoothly, uninterrupted by decreases. Rather than going along 4 visible raglan 'seams', the spread of decreases differ on alternate decrease rounds, to mask the decreases and avoid them forming 'seams' on the RS.

Round 1 (dec): *SspA&B, [p31 (36, 39, 23, 25, 28)A&B, sspA&B] x 1 (1, 1, 2, 2, 2), [p31 (36, 39, 23, 25, 28)A&B, p2togA&B] x 1 (1, 1, 2, 2, 2), p33 (37, 41, 27, 29, 31)A&B, p2togA&B, work 23 (23, 23, 33, 33, 33) sts as set*.
Repeat from * to * once more. (8 (8, 8, 12, 12, 12) sts dec)
244 (272, 292, 316, 336, 364) sts

Round 2 and all even rounds: Work straight as set.

Round 3 (dec): *P23 (17, 19, 30, 32, 36)A&B, [p2togA&B, p49 (36, 40, 61, 67, 73)A&B] x 1 (2, 2, 1, 1, 1), sspA&B, p23 (18, 18, 30, 32, 36)A&B, work 23 (23, 23, 33, 33, 33) as set*.
Repeat from * to * once more. (4 (6, 6, 4, 4, 4) sts dec)
240 (266, 286, 312, 332, 360) sts

Round 5 (dec): *SspA&B, [p29 (34, 37, 22, 24, 27)A&B, sspA&B] x 1 (1, 1, 2, 2, 2), [p29 (34, 37, 22, 24, 27)A&B, p2togA&B] x 1 (1, 1, 2, 2, 2), p31 (34, 38, 23, 25, 27)A&B, p2togA&B, work 23 (23, 23, 33, 33, 33) as set*.
Repeat from * to * once more. (8 (8, 8, 12, 12, 12) sts dec)
232 (258, 278, 300, 320, 348) sts

Round 7 (dec): *P22 (15, 17, 28, 30, 34)A&B, [p2togA&B, p45 (35, 38, 57, 63, 69)A&B] x 1 (2, 2, 1, 1, 1), sspA&B, p22 (15, 17, 28, 30, 34)A&B, work 23 (23, 23, 33, 33, 33) as set*.
Repeat from * to * once more.
(4 (6, 6, 4, 4, 4) sts dec) *228 (252, 272, 296, 316, 344) sts*

Round 9 (dec): *SspA&B, [p27 (31, 35, 20, 22, 25)A&B, sspA&B] x 1 (1, 1, 2, 2, 2), [p27 (31, 35, 20, 22, 25)A&B, p2togA&B] x 1 (1, 1, 2, 2, 2), p29 (33, 35, 23, 25, 27)A&B, p2togA&B, work 23 (23, 23, 33, 33, 33) as set*.
Repeat from * to * once more. (8 (8, 8, 12, 12, 12) sts dec)
220 (244, 264, 284, 304, 332) sts

Round 11 (dec): *P20 (15, 15, 26, 28, 32)A&B, [p2togA&B, p43 (31, 36, 53, 59, 65)A&B] x 1 (2, 2, 1, 1, 1), sspA&B, p20 (16, 16, 26, 28, 32)A&B, work 23 (23, 23, 33, 33, 33) as set*.
Repeat from * to * once more.
(4 (6, 6, 4, 4, 4) sts dec) *216 (238, 258, 280, 300, 328) sts*

Round 13 (dec): *SspA&B, [p25 (29, 32, 19, 21, 24)A&B, sspA&B] x 1 (1, 1, 2, 2, 2), [p25 (29, 32, 19, 21, 24)A&B, p2togA&B] x 1 (1, 1, 2, 2, 2), p27 (30, 34, 19, 21, 23)A&B, p2togA&B, work 23 (23, 23, 33, 33, 33) as set*.
Repeat from * to * once more. (8 (8, 8, 12, 12, 12) sts dec)
208 (230, 250, 268, 288, 316) sts

Round 15 (dec): *P18 (14, 15, 24, 26, 30)A&B, [p2togA&B, p41 (29, 33, 49, 55, 61)A&B] x 1 (2, 2, 1, 1, 1), sspA&B, p18 (14, 15, 24, 26, 30)A&B, work 23 (23, 23, 33, 33, 33) as set*.
Repeat from * to * once more. (4 (6, 6, 4, 4, 4) sts dec)
204 (224, 244, 264, 284, 312) sts

Round 17 (dec): *SspA&B, [p23 (27, 30, 17, 19, 22)A&B, sspA&B] x 1 (1, 1, 2, 2, 2), [p23 (27, 30, 17, 19, 22)A&B, p2togA&B] x 1 (1, 1, 2, 2, 2), p25 (27, 31, 19, 21, 23)A&B, p2togA&B, work 23 (23, 23, 33, 33, 33) as set*.
Repeat from * to * once more.
(8 (8, 8, 12, 12, 12) sts dec) *196 (216, 236, 252, 272, 300) sts*

Round 19 (dec): *P17 (14, 14, 22, 25, 28)A&B, [p2togA&B, p(37 (26, 30, 45, 49, 57)A&B] x 1 (2, 2, 1, 1, 1), sspA&B, p17 (13, 15, 22, 25, 28)A&B, work 23 (23, 23, 33, 33, 33) as set*.
Repeat from * to * once more. (4 (6, 6, 4, 4, 4) sts dec)
192 (210, 230, 248, 268, 296) sts

short rows.

On alternate even rounds, between the uneven-numbered decrease rounds, you will now work short rows. Even rounds that are not short rows should be worked straight as set. The short rows are in a sense optional, as the rounds can be worked 'as set' if you don't fancy them, but they are highly recommended for a superior fit. Though w&t short rows are specified, use the method you prefer, such as Sunday Short Rows. Remember to carry the floats of Yarn A on the WS when you are working the WS of Centre Back DS on a short row.

Round 21 (dec): *SspA&B, [p21 (24, 28, 16, 18, 20)A&B, sspA&B] x 1 (1, 1, 2, 2, 2), [p21 (24, 28, 16, 18, 20)A&B, p2togA&B] x 1 (1, 1, 2, 2, 2), p23 (26, 28, 15, 17, 23)A&B, p2togA&B, work 23 (23, 23, 33, 33, 33) as set*.
Repeat from * to * once more. (8 (8, 8, 12, 12, 12) st dec)
184 (202, 222, 236, 256, 284) sts

Round 22 (short row): Work 158 (176, 196, 200, 220, 248) sts in pattern, to 3 sts before MZ, w&t round following st, work WS in pattern as set for 155 (173, 193, 197, 217, 245) sts to 3 sts before MW, w&t round following st, work to end of round, working wrap with the wrapped st as you pass it.

Note: Remember to work the wrap with the wrapped st as you pass it in the next round (the wrapped one you haven't attended to before). You will need to do this every time you work a short row.

Round 23 (dec): ★P16 (12, 13, 20, 22, 27)A&B, [p2togA&B, p33 (24, 28, 41, 47, 51)A&B] x 1 (2, 2, 1, 1, 1), sspA&B, p16 (12, 13, 20, 22, 27)A&B, work 23 (23, 23, 33, 33, 33) as set★. Repeat from ★ to ★ once more. (4 (6, 6, 4, 4, 4) sts dec)
180 (196, 216, 232, 252, 280) sts

Round 24 and all even rounds unless specified as short rows: Work straight as set.

Round 25 (dec): ★SspA&B, [p19 (22, 25, 14, 16, 19)A&B, sspA&B] x 1 (1, 1, 2, 2, 2), [p19 (22, 25, 14, 16, 19)A&B, p2togA&B] x 1 (1, 1, 2, 2, 2), p21 (23, 27, 15, 17, 19)A&B, p2togA&B, work 23 (23, 23, 33, 33, 33) as set★. Repeat from ★ to ★ once more. (8 (8, 8, 12, 12, 12) sts dec)
172 (188, 208, 220, 240, 268) sts

Round 26 (short row): Work 142 (158, 178, 180, 200, 228) sts in pattern, to 7 sts before MZ, w&t round following st, work WS in pattern as set for 135 (151, 171, 173, 193, 221) sts to 7 sts before MW, w&t round following st, work to end of round, working wrap with the wrapped st as you pass it.

Round 27 (dec): ★P14 (11, 12, 18, 21, 25)A&B, [p2togA&B, p31 (21, 25, 37, 41, 47)A&B] x 1 (2, 2, 1, 1, 1), sspA&B, p14 (12, 13, 18, 21, 25)A&B, work 23 (23, 23, 33, 33, 33) as set★. Repeat from ★ to ★ once more. (4 (6, 6, 4, 4, 4) sts dec)
168 (182, 202, 216, 236, 264) sts

Round 29 (dec): ★SspA&B, [p17 (20, 23, 12, 14, 17)A&B, sspA&B] x 1 (1, 1, 2, 2, 2), [p17 (20, 23, 12, 14, 17)A&B, p2togA&B] x 1 (1, 1, 2, 2, 2), p19 (20, 24, 15, 17, 19)A&B, p2togA&B, work 23 (23, 23, 33, 33, 33) as set★. Repeat from ★ to ★ once more. (8 (8, 8, 12, 12, 12) sts dec)
160 (174, 194, 204, 224, 252) sts

Round 30 (short row): Work 126 (140, 160, 160, 180, 208) sts in pattern, to 11 sts before MZ, w&t round following st, work WS in pattern as set for 115 (129, 149, 149, 169, 197) sts to 11 sts before MW, w&t round following st, work to end of round, working wrap with the wrapped st as you pass it.

Round 31 (dec): ★P13 (11, 11, 17, 19, 23)A&B, [p2togA&B, p27 (19, 23, 31, 37, 43)A&B] x 1 (2, 2, 1, 1, 1), sspA&B, p13 (9, 11, 17, 19, 23)A&B, work 23 (23, 23, 33, 33, 33) as set★. Repeat from ★ to ★ once more. (4 (6, 6, 4, 4, 4) sts dec)
156 (168, 188, 200, 220, 248) sts

Round 33 (dec): ★SspA&B, [p15 (17, 21, 11, 13, 16)A&B, sspA&B] x 1 (1, 1, 2, 2, 2), [p15 (17, 21, 11, 13, 16)A&B, p2togA&B] x 1 (1, 1, 2, 2, 2), p17 (19, 21, 11, 13, 15)A&B, p2togA&B, work 23 (23, 23, 33, 33, 33) as set★. Repeat from ★ to ★ once more. (8 (8, 8, 12, 12, 12) sts dec)
148 (160, 180, 188, 208, 236) sts

Round 34 (short row): Work 110 (122, 142, 140, 160, 188) sts in pattern, to 15 sts before MZ, w&t round following st, work WS in pattern as set for 95 (107, 127, 125, 145, 173) sts to 15 sts before MW, w&t round following st, work to end of round, working wrap with the wrapped st as you pass it.

Round 35 (dec): ★P11 (9, 11, 15, 18, 21)A&B, [p2togA&B, p25 (17, 20, 27, 31, 39)A&B] x 1 (2, 2, 1, 1, 1), sspA&B, p11 (8, 10, 15, 18, 21)A&B, work 23 (23, 23, 33, 33, 33) as set★. Repeat from ★ to ★ once more. (4 (6, 6, 4, 4, 4) sts dec)
144 (154, 174, 184, 204, 232) sts

Round 37 (dec): ★SspA&B, [p13 (15, 18, 9, 11, 14)A&B, sspA&B] x 1 (1, 1, 2, 2, 2), [p13 (15, 18, 9, 11, 14)A&B, p2togA&B] x 1 (1, 1, 2, 2, 2), p15 (16, 20, 11, 13, 15)A&B, p2togA&B, work 23 (23, 23, 33, 33, 33) as set★. Repeat from ★ to ★ once more. (8 (8, 8, 12, 12, 12) sts dec)
136 (146, 166, 172, 192, 220) sts

Round 38 (short row): Work 95 (105, 125, 121, 141, 169) sts in pattern, to 18 sts before MZ, w&t round following st, work WS in pattern as set for 77 (87, 107, 103, 123, 151) sts to 18 sts before MW, w&t round following st, work to end of round, working wrap with the wrapped st as you pass it.

Round 39 (dec): ★P10 (6, 8, 12, 15, 18)A&B, [p2togA&B, p21 (16, 19, 25, 29, 37)A&B] x 1 (2, 2, 1, 1, 1), sspA&B, p10 (6, 8, 12, 15, 18)A&B, work 23 (23, 23, 33, 33, 33) as set★. Repeat from ★ to ★ once more. (4 (6, 6, 4, 4, 4) sts dec)
132 (140, 160, 168, 188, 216) sts

Round 41 (dec): ★SspA&B, [p11 (13, 16, 8, 10, 12)A&B, sspA&B] x 1 (1, 1, 2, 2, 2), [p11 (13, 16, 8, 10, 12)A&B, p2togA&B] x 1 (1, 1, 2, 2, 2), p13 (13, 17, 7, 9, 15)A&B, p2togA&B, work 23 (23, 23, 33, 33, 33) as set★. Repeat from ★ to ★ once more. (8 (8, 8, 12, 12, 12) sts dec)
124 (132, 152, 156, 176, 204) sts

Round 42 (short row): Work 81 (89, 109, 103, 123, 151) sts in

pattern, to 20 sts before MZ, w&t round following st, work WS in pattern as set for 61 (69, 89, 83, 103, 131) sts to 20 sts before MW, w&t round following st, work to end of round, working wrap with the wrapped st as you pass it.

Round 43 (dec): ★P9 (5, 7, 11, 13, 17)A&B, [p2togA&B, p8 (14, 17, 19, 25, 31)A&B] x 2 (2, 2, 1, 1, 1), noting the extra repeat worked in size XS in this instance, sspA&B, p8 (4, 6, 11, 13, 17) A&B, work 23 (23, 23, 33, 33, 33) as set★. Repeat from ★ to ★ once more. (6 (6, 6, 4, 4, 4) sts dec) *118 (126, 146, 152, 172, 200) sts*

Size XS Body is complete after Round 43.
Time to work the Funnel Neck for this size.

Sizes S-XXL ONLY
Round 45 (dec): ★SspA&B, [p- (11, 14, 6, 8, 11)A&B, sspA&B] x - (1, 1, 2, 2, 2), [p- (11, 14, 6, 8, 11)A&B, p2togA&B] x - (1, 1, 2, 2, 2), p- (10, 14, 7, 9, 11)A&B, p2togA&B, work - (23, 23, 33, 33, 33) as set★. Repeat from ★ to ★ once more. (- (8, 8, 12, 12, 12) sts dec) - *(118, 138, 140, 160, 188) sts*

Size S Body is complete after Round 45.
Time to work the Funnel Neck for this size.

Sizes M-XXL ONLY
Round 47 (dec): ★SspA&B, [p- (-, 13, 5, 7, 10)A&B, sspA&B] x - (-, 1, 2, 2, 2), [p- (-, 13, 5, 7, 10)A&B, p2togA&B] x - (-, 1, 2, 2, 2), p- (-, 12, 5, 7, 9)A&B, p2togA&B, work - (-, 23, 33, 33, 33) as set★. Repeat from ★ to ★ once more. (- (-, 8, 12, 12, 12) sts dec) - *(-, 130, 128, 148, 176) sts*

Round 49 (dec): ★SspA&B, [p- (-, -, 8, 8, 6, 8)A&B, sspA&B] x - (-, 2, 1, 2, 2), [p- (-, -, 8, 8, 6, 8)A&B, p2togA&B] x - (-, 1, 1, 2, 2), p- (-, -, 8, 7, 5, 11)A&B, p2togA&B, work - (-, 23, 33, 33, 33) as set★. Repeat from ★ to ★ once more. (- (-, 10, 8, 12, 12) sts dec) - *(-, 120, 120, 136, 164) sts*

Sizes M and L Body are complete after Round 49.
Time to work the Funnel Neck for these sizes.

Sizes XL and XXL ONLY
Round 51 (dec): ★SspA&B, [p- (-, -, -, 4, 7) (A&B, sspA&B] x 2, [p- (-, -, -, 4, 7)A&B, p2togA&B] x 2, p- (-, -, -, 7, 9)A&B, p2togA&B, work 33 sts as set★. Repeat from ★ to ★ once more. (12 sts dec) - *(-, -, -, 124, 152) sts*

Round 52: Work straight as set.

Size XL Body is complete after Round 52.
Time to work the Funnel Neck for this size.

Size XXL ONLY
Round 53 (dec): ★SspA&B, [p6A&B, sspA&B] x 2, [p6A&B, p2togA&B] twice, p7A&B, p2togA&B, work 33 sts as set★. Repeat from ★ to ★ once more. (12 sts dec) - *(-, -, -, -, 140) sts*

Round 55 (dec): ★SspA&B, [p5A&B, sspA&B] twice, [p5A&B, p2togA&B] twice, p5A&B, p2togA&B, work 33 sts as set★. Repeat from ★ to ★ once more. (12 sts dec) *128 sts*

Round 56: Work straight as set.

Size XXL Body is complete after Round 56.
Time to work the Funnel Neck for this size.

all sizes again.
118 (118, 120, 120, 124, 128) sts

funnel neck.
Worked in garter stitch with the FDS and Centre Back DS maintained all the way until the sweater is complete.

Note: Though it seems counterintuitive to cast off sts just to pick the same number of sts up again, the reason for this seam is that it helps keep the shape of the garment, preventing the neckline from over-stretching with wear and the weight of the sweater below it. It also makes the Funnel Neck stand up a little more. Because you are transitioning to garter stitch (for extra structure), the seam should be near-invisible from the outside. The FDS is not cast off, so that it runs more smoothly without the pick up and knit. However, this does allow the FDS to have stretch the rest of the neckline doesn't. If you would prefer your decorative lines to run straight, then also cast off across the FDS.

Next Round: Leave BOR marker in place, remove other markers as you go. Using both yarns, purl to cast off 46 (46, 47, 42, 44, 46) sts to Centre Back DS. Slip last st you cast off plus the next 3 Centre Back DS sts (without knitting them) on to a stitch holder and leave at RS of work. Allow the yarn you are casting off with to float behind these 4 held sts. Purl to cast off 46 (46, 47, 42, 44, 46) sts to FDS. Leave final cast-off st on needle. Work FDS. Do not break yarns. *28 (28, 28, 38, 38, 38) sts*

Next Round: Using smaller needles and both yarns, pick up and knit 45 (45, 46, 41, 43, 45) sts, slide 4 held sts back into action, k1A&B, k3B for Centre Back DS, pick up and knit 45 (45, 46, 41, 43, 45) sts. Knit final cast-off st using A&B, then work FDS. *118 (118, 120, 120, 124, 128) sts*

Round 1 (Neck Round): P46 (46, 47, 42, 44, 46)A&B, k3B for Centre Back DS, p46 (46, 47, 42, 44, 46)A&B, FDS.
Round 2 (Knit Round): K46 (46, 47, 42, 44, 46)A&B, k3B for Centre Back DS, k46 (46, 47, 42, 44, 46)A&B, FDS.

Repeat Rounds 1–2 for garter stitch with Centre Back DS and FDS until you've worked a total of 22 (22, 24, 24, 26, 26) rounds. Work Round 1 once more, for a total of 12 (12, 13, 13, 14, 14) garter ridges.

Break Yarn A, leaving a tail long enough to weave in later.

cast off.

Using larger needles and Yarn B, kfb the first st and cast these 2 sts off on themselves to leave 1 st (this is a trick to avoid the dip the start of a cast-off usually creates, which is especially useful in high-visibility places), knit to cast off till you reach the FDS, then [k3, p2], k3 the FDS as you cast off.

special finishing instructions.

Ensure FDS and Centre Back DS are straight when blocking and that the fold between the Front and Back of the garment runs vertically along the central stitch of the Left and Right Side DSs. Ease the Funnel Neck into shape, remembering that the back neckline should be higher than the front because of the short rows. See General Finishing Instructions on page 142 for additional guidance.

RUPERTO

/ˈruːpətəʊ/

Like cricket and Sunday roasts, Rupert the Bear belongs to an idea of Britishness that my family just isn't part of. But my childhood neighbours were. I used to spend a lot of time over there before I became a teenager. It was the 1980s, they had a vintage MG sports car that was kept in a lock-up garage and was tinkered with on weekends. In their living room was a poster of David Hockney's *Mr and Mrs Clark and Percy* (his 1970–71 portrait of the fabric designer Celia Birtwell and her husband, the dress designer Ossie Clark, with their white cat, Percy, on his knee). My neighbours' kitchen shelves were lined with vintage Oxo tins, Cornishware, Clarice Cliff teaware and Marmite jars. There seemed to be an endless supply of KitKats, Penguin biscuits, Club bars, and Mr Kipling cakes. The children didn't have to eat their crusts and their skin burnt easily in the sun. Alongside Rupert Bear, there was *The Beano* and *Mandy* or *Bunty* to be read, while Eric Clapton and Pink Floyd cassette tapes played.

Very occasionally, in my people-watching adventures around London, I see a gentlemanly type wearing a classic Rupert the Bear scarf; its yellow and black woven checks are striking and instantly recognisable. Because of its familiarity, the brightness is lessened, even against otherwise sombre attire. It is part of the fabric of the nation. However, those who grew up with Rupert are ageing in a way the fictional character never will, though he has become dated. Rupert has gone through many changes in what is considered socially acceptable or desirable for children to see. Multiculturalism and other forms of equality are a much more explicit goal now, especially in children's literature for those who want the next generation to grow up to be open-minded individuals. Times have changed: Rupert characters such as Pong-Ping the Pekingese now send up a red flag, others such as Golliwog are hard to explain to kids now — and Rupert no longer visits Coon Island in quite the same way. Indeed, the most recent animated version (aimed at a very young audience) saw a number of the historically male central characters become female and others added, to fill what had become a visible void. In an interesting branding split, The Rupert Annual is still a yearly publication for the more mature traditionalist. It would appear that sensitivity is needed both ways. The classic Rupert remains a reflection of bygone eras, in the same way that things we do now will inevitably seem inappropriate, incomprehensible or simply quaint in the future. Erasing Rupert's past isn't necessarily all that helpful, it is an important reminder that things can change.

Though it's taken a bear-sized step away, this scarf was inspired by Rupert's. The sizing of the blocks mimics his bold muffler, but the Marlisle reduces the punch of yellow, making the dark more dominant. A way to bring it into the future as a reference, rather than a homage. This pattern is, of course, named after the iconic bear, but by adding the 'o' at the end, it also becomes named after an artist friend of mine whose last name is Ruperto. I like connecting the fictive bear character who has a complicated heritage to a conceptually driven, creative friend who has a deep appreciation of complicated layers of meaning. That he was born in the Philippines and we met in the USA satisfyingly moves things away from provincial, middle class, British whiteness to base Rupert/o in a diversity that is more current.

yarn pairing notes.

To reference Rupert's Britishness, the yarns specified in this project are British, but what unites them more closely is that they are both strongly linked to Scotland. If we are thinking about the complications of national identity through yarns and the role of a single country

of origin, bear in mind that Scotland used to be a sovereign nation and may one day be one again. The 2014 referendum on Scottish independence was very close. There were those, often fuelled by a connection to specifically inherited national identity, who voted for or against independence with an eye to rectifying or maintaining historic wrongs. But the uncertainty of whether an independent Scotland would be allowed to stay part of the European Union was a sticking point for many. In hindsight, this strategy may have been in vain, as the UK had a referendum in 2016 and as a result looks likely at the time of going to print to be on course to leave the European Union.... National borders and rights of access are constantly shifting, which makes them a tricky thing to base yarn provenance on, if we do not want it to be about nationalism.

These two Scottish yarns are DK/light worsted, but beyond that they are very different in character. The Ryeland is a sturdy, round, densely plied yarn that softens significantly with washing and wearing. It is spun at the Natural Fibre Company mill from a coloured flock of pedigree Ryeland sheep, whose fleeces are selected for their different shades. If you should happen to purchase Rosedean Ryelands yarn online, the payment will go to The Accidental Smallholder Ltd, a fact that tickled me maybe more than any small print at the bottom of a receipt ever has. I felt an affinity. I instantly imagined Rosemary and Dan Champion considering getting sheep and going to the market in the name of research. Once there, one thing lead to another, they fell in love with a Ryeland and accidentally came home with a sheep. That ewe seemed lonely, so a second was added, and from there their introduction to farming gathered pace.

Travel a little south-west of Carnoustie, Angus, where the Rosedean flock grazes and you might find yourself in beautiful Edinburgh. If you're in search of a taste of the city's woolly flavour, stop by Ginger Twist Studio: it is the tiniest of yarn shops you can imagine. It is perfect: dreamy and cosy, crowded if there are four people in there. Filled with an admirable selection of local and yarns from farther afield and an eye-catching wall of hand-dyed skeins hanging, unfurled, from pegs. It is owned by Jessica James-Thomson, who you are likely to find sitting in the centre of it all on her knitting throne, channelling some old-fashioned glamour with her cat-eye frames and a WIP. Her Ginger's Hand Dyed Masham Mayhem base is a combination of Bluefaced Leicester and Masham. In comparison with the Ryeland, it is thinner, but what it lacks in solid girth it more than makes up for with it's halo of loosely spun softness.

Knitted scarves should wrap around a neck easily and hang nicely, yet not be so floppy that it loses shape and distorts. Two soft, slippery yarns would result in a flimsy scarf, whereas two yarns with a fiercer structure create too much bulk when worn around the neck. If substituting yarns, you should aim for pairing of two different types: one with more 'give' and the other with less or two somewhere in the middle in terms of structure. It's fun to feel the different properties of the specified yarns running through your fingers as you knit. The combo creates a dense, springy fabric with a satisfying level of drape.

construction and fit.

This scarf is long enough to be worn wrapped around your neck once, or doubled with both ends pulled through, depending on how you like to style your neckwear. The stitch pattern was carefully designed to make the fabric reversible - not the same on both sides, but interesting on both sides. It's a personal bugbear (rather than Rupert the Bear) of mine when scarves and shawls only have one considered side, with the other one being purely consequential or ideally, concealed.

The Ruperto scarf is knitted in the round, lengthwise, thanks to a steek section that is cut once all the knitting is complete. It uses the same knotted steek found in the Ess Shawl (page 84) and Shantay Cardigan (page 54). The stitches you unravel from the steek section are knotted to form the fringing, leaving no ends to weave in. The other perk of the steek is that it alleviates the need to worry whether you have a twist in your circular knit. It simply doesn't matter if the scarf is worked as an unintentional helix, as you'll be cutting it in half anyway (which will undo any untoward twists and turns). Luckily, too, because casting on 255 stitches is nothing to be sneezed at or repeated accidentally owing to error. The replacement thing-to-watch-out-for, as with any sideways-knitted scarf, is that your cast-on and cast-off have the same amount of give or you'll end up with a scarf that hangs like a banana.

sizing.

ONE SIZE

Designed to be worn wrapped around neck once, or doubled with both ends pulled through.

yarn.

Yarn A: Rosedean Ryelands, DK (DK/light worsted; 100% Ryeland; 110m/120yds per 50g/1¾oz)
Dark (2016) x 3

Yarn B: Ginger's Hand Dyed, Masham Mayhem (DK/light worsted; 75% Bluefaced Leicester, 25% Masham; 240m/262yds per 100g/3½oz)
Muddy Sunshine x 1

Yarn quantity note: The quantity of Yarn B is close, without being ridiculously so. If you tend to gobble yarn and don't like playing yarn chicken, either buy a second skein or you can omit one 20-st repeat of the pattern, to only work it 11 times across the round. In this case, cast on 222 sts using the crochet method for a total of 235 sts. Your scarf will be slightly shorter, but still plenty long enough. Conversely, if you have plenty of yarn and want a longer scarf (to satisfy your inner Doctor Who), you can add additional multiples of 20 sts to the cast-on according to the length you would like.

worn by...

Vonnie (and **Adam**) in Dark and Muddy Sunshine, knitted by Mandy Hewett. The red coat worn by Vonnie is sewn by Marilla Walker from her Honetone pattern.

gauge.

14 stitches x 29 rounds = 10cm x 10cm/4" x 4" over garter stitch with both yarns held together after blocking.

Swatching note: Because you will cast on 242 sts for the actual scarf, it would be wise to be happy with your gauge before that. However grudgingly you feel towards not getting started on the actual scarf straight-away, this means doing a swatch, and ideally a circular one (to get the truest indication of gauge). This will also allow you to test that your cast-on and cast-off have the same level of stretchiness (which will avoid a scarf that hangs like a banana).

Using Yarn A and the crochet method, cast on 40 sts, join in the round, being careful not to twist. Work the 20-st boxed repeat of the Ruperto chart twice across the round. Work to end of Ruperto chart row repeat, then cast off kwise using Yarn A only. Don't secure ends tightly, so that you can undo your swatch if you need the yarn to finish the scarf.

needles.

6mm (US10) circular needle, 100cm/40".
5.5mm (USI/9) crochet hook for working crochet method cast-on.

Always use a needle size that will result in the correct gauge after blocking.

notions.

stitch marker – you may find 2 useful
tapestry needle
small sharp scissors for cutting steek
long-bladed fabric scissors (if you have them) to trim fringe

pattern notes.

Cast-on/off: The crochet method is specified for the main cast-on, because it pairs nicely with a standard cast-off and is reversible. The cable method is a good alternative to the crochet method for casting on, but it has a more distinct RS and WS, and doesn't pair quite as well with a standard cast-off. Whatever cast-on and yarn you choose to use, you are aiming for something that will have the same level of stretchiness as the cast-off you use, so that you don't get a lopsided scarf.

Steek section: The 13-st steek section is knitted every round, according to Columns 23-35 at the end of the chart. You use Yarn A&B held together for the 6 first and last sts and a single Yarn B stitch in the centre for Column 29 (which will be your guideline for cutting along), except for Rows 9-11, 22-24 and 35-37 where you will use Yarn A only and leave Yarn B resting at the end of Rows 8, 21 and 34 until you need it again for Rows 12, 25 and 38.

How to slip stitches: Always slip the sts (in Columns 1-2 and 11-12 of the boxed repeat and Column 21-22 after the repeats) purlwise, so they don't twist. You will be slipping the same sts on 3 consecutive rounds, so they will have a tendency to get a little bit misshapen. If this bothers you, disperse any slack across neighbouring sts with the tip of your needle.

Alternating balls of yarn when there's a steek section:
Unless you are entirely confident your dye lots are identical, it's worth alternating rounds of the new and old balls to avoid any difference between them affecting the overall look. If, however, you are convinced your dye lots are the same (or are happy with the transition of the differences between them), when you change from one ball of yarn to the next, either spit-splice the new and old end together (if you are in the middle of a round) or, without joining the ends in any way, place the transition of ends in the centre of the steek section. This last option will mean you don't have to join or sew in any ends at all.

schematic.

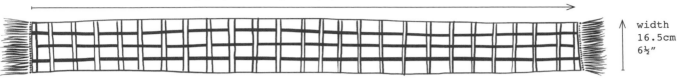

length (excluding fringe) 173cm/68"

width
16.5cm
6½"

←
fringe
7cm
2¾"

chart.

key.

▨	Worked with Yarn B only, with Yarn A held at back
☐	Worked with Yarn A&B
■	Worked with Yarn A only, with Yarn B held at back
☐	repeat
☐	knit
•	purl
V	slip purlwise

pattern begins.

Note: Make sure to use the thicker of your two yarns for the cast-on and cast-off (if there is a difference between them) to make sure it is as bulky as possible (without using both yarns). It is important to use the backwards-loop method where specified for the first 13 sts of the cast-on. These 13 sts will become the steek section. In the first row, when you work into the backwards loop cast-on, it can be a little difficult to knit into, owing to tightness, but the pay-off is that it is easy to undo at the end (when you unravel the steek section to make the fringing).

Using Yarn A and the backwards-loop method, cast on 13 sts, then, using the crochet hook and crochet method, cast on 242 more sts to bring the total to 255 sts. Do not join in the round yet.

Note: You will work the first row of the Ruperto chart flat, without joining in the round and then join to work in the round from then on. This is easier than joining in the round straight after the cast-on (less risk of twisting, as you have a couple of rows to look at). However, a benefit of working a scarf lengthwise with a steek is that if you discover you do have a twist, it is of no concern, because you will be cutting it later (which will undo the twist).

Set-up Row: Work Row 1 of Ruperto chart, working the boxed section of chart 12 times, before completing row.

Join in the round. PM to mark BOR. If it is helpful to you, place a second marker on the other side of the 13-st steek section. You will slip the markers each time you pass them.

Work Rows 2-46 of Ruperto chart, working the boxed section of chart 12 times across each round, then work to end of chart, finishing with the 13 steek sts.

Rows 9-11, 22-24 and 35-37 of Ruperto chart should be worked in Yarn A only. Stop using Yarn B, leaving it at the BOR (after working Rounds 8, 21 and 34), until you next need it to work with (to start Rounds 12, 25 and 38). Do not carry Yarn B around and do not cut it.

Break Yarn B, leaving a 10cm/4" tail. Cast off 242 sts kwise using Yarn A only. Leave 13 steek sts live on your needles. Break Yarn A, leaving a 10cm/4" tail.

special finishing instructions.

Cutting the steek: Remove the needle from the 13 remaining live steek sts. Using small, sharp scissors, cut down the centre of the 13 steek sts along your single-colour st guideline (Column 29) to leave 6.5 sts on either side, from the live sts and through the backwards-loop cast-on. You now have a long scarf with two distinct edges, rather than a loop. Work on each edge of the scarf individually from now on.

Unravelling and knotting the steek: Starting at the edge with live sts, 2 rounds at a time, unravel the 6.5 sts in both yarns used. (Rather than unravelling the whole steek section straight away and risking the confusion of which strands to knot together afterwards, only unravel the ends you will tie together in the next knot.) Tie a basic overhand knot with the 4 ends of yarn and push it snugly to the edge of the pattern zone. Make sure the knot is pushed right up to the Yarn B stripe from Columns 1-2 and 21-22 of the chart, but not so tight that it distorts it. By using this edge as a guide, all the knots will be nice and consistently placed. You will need to fudge the number of ends you tie together a little around the Yarn A-only stripes in Rounds 9-11, 22-24 and 35-37. Do this to your liking: you can either make a Yarn A-only knot here or spread the Yarn A ends out to the neighbouring knots, which will mean you have only 3 strands in some, but can make them using Yarn A&B along the whole edge. If you would like all your tassels to contain both colours, loop in extra strands of Yarn B where you were only using Yarn A to knit with. To do this, cut a 20cm/8" strand from your left-over Yarn B and, with the help of a crochet hook, pull through the space between the rows so that half sticks out each side. Tie it into the knot with the strands of Yarn A from the steek.

Blocking the scarf: When all the knots are tied, it's time for a good soak in your favourite wool-friendly detergent. Leave it to soak for a good half an hour or more to allow the kinks in the fringing to relax and the stitches to ease into place. Rinse and squeeze out water. Do not wring. Wrap in a towel and sit or stand on it to squish out excess moisture. Allow to dry flat, using plenty of pins, to avoid scalloped edges. If you have them, blocking wires threaded up the long edges will help you achieve a straighter edge with less pins. Use your fingers to 'comb' out the fringing (or use a very wide-toothed comb or fork) so that it dries flat and straight.

Trimming the fringe: Once dry, comb the fringing again. Before unpinning (so that the scarf is supported and stable), trim the fringing to 7cm/2¾" (or longer/shorter, depending on your preference). Using fabric scissors with long, sharp blades (if you have them) helps keep things straight and resist additional fidget snipping. Start longer than you want the fringe to allow yourself to get shorter (and shorter) as you finesse the straightness of your edge.

The shapes in this cowl are made up of rounds of tessellating diamonds, arranged to form rows of chevrons. As a word, chevron has its etymological roots in *chèvre*, the French word for goat. This probably stems from the fact that this triangular shape looks like one end or the other of a goat — either the horns or the distinctly angular back legs. Unlike sheep, which are known for their timid, flock nature (a nature that is considered undesirable in humans), goats have fulfilled a very different role in popular culture.

In stories, they are by turn stubborn or spritely. Half-human as satyrs, they are variously characterised as lusty, demonic and musical. And they are elsewhere celebrated for their child-rearing skills by lending their name to 'nanny' — appropriate for this cowl, because it too will envelope you in protective warmth.

yarn pairing notes.

One goat reference deserves another and mohair comes from Angora goats (not to be confused with fibre from Angora rabbits, which produce angora). Yeavering Bell yarn from Whistlebare is made of a combo of fibre from the Angora goats and Wensleydale sheep raised by Alice Elsworth and her family on their farm in picturesque Berwick-upon-Tweed in Northumberland, the most northerly county in England. It is lustrous and strong, thanks to being worsted-spun and then plied from this combination of long-stapled fleeces at Laxton's, in Yorkshire, before being returned to the farm to be dyed by Alice. If your idea of mohair is the capricious, brushed 1980s sort with a high synthetic content, this is quite a different beast.

Because of the French name, a pairing with a French yarn seemed a natural choice, especially for the one that would be *au naturel*, undyed. When it comes to wool, Merino has become ubiquitous as shorthand for softness and quality. I have mostly avoided it in the collection of yarns I have used in this book, in favour of spreading the love to lesser-used breeds. However, I did want to include a couple of interesting examples of the world's favourite single-breed wool. De Rerum Natura is certainly one of them. The project of Solenn Couix-Loarer, it is woollen-spun then plied in France using fleece from three breeds she describes as MacoMérinos (raised in the Southern Alps); Mérinos d'Arles (from, you guessed it, Provence, near Arles); and Mérinos noirs Petra from the Alentejo Valley in Portugal. Unlike the pure white Merinos we are used to envisaging in the epic flocks of Australia, New Zealand and South Africa, the Portuguese flock lend a greater variety of colour to the undyed shade options for this cowl. It is a squooshy and round yarn, with great stitch definition.

construction and fit.

It's hard to think of a simpler garment to knit in the round than a cowl. The ease of no shaping lets you focus on working the striking stitch pattern, which requires attention, without being overly complicated. Because of the different characters of the yarns used, the shapes gently float, dancing and hovering with a mind of their own, rather than the regimented chevrons associated with military rank badges. It's not a deep cowl, but has been designed to be just long enough to keep you warm, while not obscuring the stitch pattern in the folds that would appear if you made it longer. You can of course make it as long as you have enough yarn for.

To provide you with an idea of which size to choose, guidance is given of how it is intended to fit around the ears, as these are likely to be the widest point of your head and neck. From this you can ascertain whether you would like a snug or wide-fitting cowl. The range of sizes offered makes it easy to substitute different yarn weights (if you're prepared to play around with finding the correct gauge for your chosen yarn combo). Generally, if you use thinner yarn, use smaller needles and the instructions for the larger size. If you use thicker yarn, use bigger needles and the smaller cowl size instructions.

sizing.

S (M, L)
Designed to be worn with slight positive ease when measuring around the ears.

yarn.

Yarn A: De Rerum Natura, Gilliatt (aran/worsted; 100% Merino; 250m/273yds per 100g/3½oz)
Poivre Blanc or Poivre et Sel x 1

Yarn B: Whistlebare, Yeavering Bell Aran (aran/worsted; 80% Mohair, 20% Wensleydale; 175m/190yds per 100g/3½oz)
Great Oak or Sloe Velvet x 1

With the suggested quantities, you should have enough Yarn A left over to make a second cowl in any size, in order to have enough Yarn B, you need to make two size Ss.

worn by...

Anna in Poivre et Sel and Sloe Velvet, size M, knitted by Anna Maltz. The denim coat is sewn by Marilla Walker from her Honetone pattern.
Adam in Poivre Blanc and Great Oak, size M, knitted by Rachel Rawlins. The beige coat is sewn by Marilla Walker from her Honetone pattern.

gauge.

20 stitches x 26 rounds = 10cm x 10cm/4" x 4" over Chevre stitch pattern after blocking.

needles.

5mm (US8) circular needles, 60cm/24".

Always use a needle size that will result in the correct gauge after blocking.

notions.

tapestry needle
stitch marker

glossary.

CHEVRE REPEAT
(worked in the round over multiple of 10 sts)
Round 1: [P5A&B, k5A] to end.
Round 2: [P5A&B, k1A&B, k4A] to end.
Round 3: [P4A&B, k1B, p1A&B, k1A&B, k3A] to end.
Round 4: [P3A&B, k2B, p2A&B, k1A&B, k2A] to end.
Round 5: [P2A&B, k3B, p3A&B, k1A&B, k1A] to end.
Round 6: [P1A&B, k4B, p4A&B, k1A&B] to end.
Rounds 7-9: [K5B, p5A&B] to end.
Round 10: [K4B, k1A&B, p5A&B] to end.
Round 11: [K3B, k1A&B, p1A&B, k1A, p4A&B] to end.
Round 12: [K2B, k1A&B, p2A&B, k2A, p3A&B] to end.
Round 13: [K1B, k1A&B, p3A&B, k3A, p2A&B] to end.
Round 14: [K1A&B, p4A&B, k4A, p1A&B] to end.
Rounds 15-16: [P5A&B, k5A] to end.

Note: The single sts that are knitted (rather than purled) with A&B in Rounds 2-6 and 10-14 are necessary for a smooth transition between the colour and texture changes.

pattern notes.

Cast-on: Usually it is wise to cast on with the darker of the two colours you are pairing together (whatever shows dirt the least, as it will be right at the edge). However, in combos of different weight yarns, always cast on with the heavier/rounder/sturdier of the two to ensure it takes up enough space.

Floats: The floats at the back of this cowl span 5 sts. On the first and last rounds of the cowl only, catch the Yarn B float behind the Yarn A st from Column 8 of every repeat, as instructed, to stop floats popping out and showing on the RS. Catching your float is unnecessary the remainder of the time and might interfere with the clarity of the colour on the front (and slow you down). If you feel you really must catch your floats, then make sure to vary where you catch them, to minimise how much they show up on the RS.

schematic.

circumference
50 (55, 60)cm
19¾ (21¾, 23½)"

depth
19cm
7½"

chevre repeat.

10 9 8 7 6 5 4 3 2 1

(chart grid rows numbered 1–16)

10 9 8 7 6 5 4 3 2 1

key.

☐ Worked with Yarn A&B held together

▨ Knit with Yarn A only, with Yarn B held at back

▨ Knit with Yarn B only, with Yarn A held at back

● purl

pattern begins.

Using Yarn A and the long-tail method, cast on 100 (110, 120) sts. Join in the round being careful not to twist. PM to mark BOR.

Chart note: The single sts that are knitted (rather than purled) with A&B in Rows 2-6 and 10-14 are necessary for a smooth transition between the colour and texture changes, so keep an eye out for them.

Working from Chevre Repeat chart or written instructions (see Glossary), work the 10-st repeat 10 (11, 12) times across the round, catching the Yarn B float behind the Yarn A st from Column 8 of each repeat in Round 1 only. Continue as set, working to end of 16-round repeat twice, then work Rows 1-14 only once more. Work a final Row 15 to finish, catching the Yarn B float behind the Yarn A st from Column 8 of each repeat.

Break Yarn B, leaving a tail long enough to sew in later.

Cast off using Yarn A only, purling the purl sts and knitting the knit sts (as Row 16) as you cast them off, otherwise the WS will show on the RS. See General Finishing Instructions on page 142 for guidance on what to do now.

SELBBOB

/ˈsɛlˈbɒb/

Being called Anna, with a father nicknamed Bob and a sister nick-named Sas, I have a special affinity for words spelt backwards. At secondary school, I once wrote a whole English exam essay in mirror writing. That same day, I got a note back saying:

'If you think I am going to mark this, you must be joking'.

My form tutor confided in me that it had taken my English teacher the entire lunch break, the use of a mirror and numerous pieces of paper to form that sentence and they had no idea how I had been able to write a whole essay that way in an hour with no tool to help invert the words. At least I was a creative pain in the bum.

In maths class, few numbers gave me and my fellow classmates more joy than 55378008. Sort of like a pun and a puzzle, rolled into one. I wonder what lengths students have to go to nowadays to achieve the same glee, as digital readouts no longer rely so heavily on SSD (Seven-Segment Display — think the blocky numbers used in calculators, and in LED displays to tell you when it's your turn at the counter to buy meat or postage stamps). I don't think it's just the smutty side of the early teenage brain that finds satisfaction in 55378008. I think there's a general buzz that can be derived from the transmogrification of numbers into letters: you have this one thing that you can make another thing with. A bit like yarn becoming knitting, becoming a garment. In the realm of making knitted forms out of wiggly lines of yarn, shaping bobbles gives an extra special, magical joy to my finger-tips. They are light-hearted, while being sol-idly 3D. And there is definitely something nipplish about a bobble. Perhaps bobbles should have been called boobles. So there you have it: Selbbob is 'bobbles' spelt in reverse and would be *8088735* in upside-down calculator writing.

yarn pairing notes.

My first book, *Penguin: A Knit Collection*, was dedicated to Belinda Boaden, who had passed away shortly before its publication in 2015. The hole, much larger than her diminutive form, that her absence continues to leave in the lives of many of us in the knitting community, near and far, will be a hard one to darn. She was generous and supportive with her vast knowledge, and a great community builder; a connector whose ways still reveal themselves long after her loss to cancer. The thread of this yarn pairing starts with her. In 2014, she escorted me to Wild and Woolly, which Anna Feldman had just opened. This friendly and welcoming yarn shop continues to be a place where you are likely to find me. Belinda also introduced Anna to Kim Kearney of Town End Yarns, for whom she and Wendy Baker had just designed a collection of adorable baby and toddler patterns (Wendy and Belinda worked together as True Brit Knits). Anna has stocked this wonderful, British-grown-and-spun alpaca yarn ever since. Soon she also started stocking The Wool Kitchen yarns, dyed by Helen Reed. Helen's colours and skills continue to go from strength to strength, so much so that she now has a dedicated dyeing annexe to her wool kitchen in Walthamstow, which is close enough to Wild and Woolly that she can deliver her latest dyelots by bicycle. The fluoro green, Runner, that I've used in this pattern, is dyed on her sock base, which is mainly Bluefaced Leicester with a little bamboo (a plant-based viscose alternative to petrochemi-cal synthetics). Using a sock yarn in combination with an alpaca one ensures that this hat is glori-ously soft, yet sturdy. The tightly spun sock yarn helps this hat to keep its shape when on its own

the super-softness of alpaca would have an in-clination to drape. Colour-wise, Helen and I had a long deliberation together about what would go with Runner. In the end, we opted for Town End Yarns' pale Latte, a combination that looked like it could work well, in a surprising sort of way, and I love what the colours do to each other. Runner is anything but subtle and Latte is a true classic neutral, the colour of trench coats and cashmere sweaters (and just as soft as the latter). When I decided to knit two samples for each pattern, I stuck with Runner to be able to try it in a more obvious combo, with the glorious, undyed, Rose Grey.

construction and fit.

A simple, in the round, bottom-up hat construction, zhooshed up with a corrugated rib brim and bobbles. To account for the different gauge of the yarns being worked one at a time, the brim is worked on smaller needles, which will also help keep the hat on snugly. After that, you switch to larger needles for the body and crown, which are worked in stock-ing stitch using both yarns held together. This easy-peasy background is punctuated by staggered rounds of bobbles knitted in a single colour.

This is the only instance in this collection, of a pattern where the knit side of stocking stitch is used on the front side. In the other patterns, you'll find there's always reverse stocking stitch or garter stitch as the foil for the single-coloured, knitted motifs. Because the motif on this hat is bobbly, they can't fail to 'pop' out and provide enough difference in texture, so the background doesn't need to offset them further. There's no risk that the bobbles will blend in. And because you are knitting the background of the hat using two colours held together, it is easy to choose either of the colours to use for the bobbles for another way to reverse, flip or back-to-front something in relation to this pattern. Rather than being finished off by a pompom, there is a tiny booble on top.

sizing.

S (M, L)
Designed to be worn with 5cm/2"negative ease at the brim (worn around the forehead). Size L is likely to have a slouchy fit.

yarn.

Yarn A: Town End Yarn, Pure Natural Alpaca (4ply/fingering; 100% Alpaca; 160m/175yds per 50g/1¾oz)
Latte or Rose Grey x 1

Yarn B: The Wool Kitchen, Sock (4ply/fingering; 80% Bluefaced Leicester, 20% bamboo (machine washable); 400m/437yds per 100g/3½oz)
Runner x 1

The suggested quantities should give you enough Yarn B to knit two size S hats. There is only enough Yarn A to knit one hat.

worn by...

Vonnie in Latte and Runner, size M, knitted by Anna Maltz. The pale yellow splatter-dyed top is sewn (and dyed) by Marilla Walker from her Maya pattern.
Anna in Rose Grey and Runner, size M, knitted by Vonnie Williams. The grey splatter-dyed top is sewn (and dyed) by Marilla Walker from her Maya pattern.

needles.

3.25mm (US3) for Corrugated Rib Brim.
4.5mm (US7) for Body.

Always use a needle size that will result in the correct gauge after blocking.

Needle type note: You can use either circular needles long enough for magic looping or DPNs in each size, or use 40cm/16" length circular needles for the Brim and 60cm/24" for the Body AND a pair of DPNs or magic loop in the larger size to finish.

Using needles with nice pointy tips (often called lace needles) will make the cast-offs required to form each bobble a lot easier.

gauge.

29 stitches x 42 rounds = 10cm x 10cm/4" x 4" over 3x1 Corrugated Rib on smaller needles after blocking. (For Brim.)

24 stitches x 30 rounds = 10cm x 10cm/4" x 4" over stocking stitch using both yarns held together on larger needles after blocking. (For Body.)

Swatching note: Remember to swatch in the round to get the truest indication of what size your hat will be (you can read a more extensive discussion on Swatching on page 22). The rib gauge for sts is most important to match closely, as the Corrugated Rib Brim dictates whether the hat will fit on your head.

schematic.

brim to crown
21 (22, 22)cm/8½ (8¾, 8¾)"

circumference
(widest point)
54 (58, 62)cm
21¼ (23, 24½)"

corrugated rib brim
circumference
45 (48, 51)cm
18 (19, 20)"

adapting selbbob.

If your round gauge is significantly larger/smaller, you can consider adding/removing rounds in the Corrugated Rib Brim and/or a repeat of bobbles in the Body. It is easiest to add/remove a full repeat (Rounds 1-10) of Selbbob Bobbles (2 rounds of bobbles, staggered above each other). You may wish to remove half a repeat if you are making a size L for the width of the brim, but want a less slouchy fit than the body of this hat will otherwise produce. If you try to add/remove half a repeat (1 round of bobbles) at the end of the Body, directly before working the Crown Shaping Decreases, without planning for it at the start, your bobbles will not line up between Body and Crown. You can compensate for this by adding/removing a half repeat at the beginning of the Body (after the rib), not at the end (just before crown), so that the bobbles can flow from Body to Crown as intended. To do this, for longer rounds, instead of working instructions between ★ and ★★, work Rounds 6-10 of Selbbob Bobbles chart or written instructions (see Glossary), then follow instructions from ★★ onwards to work only 6 rounds of bobbles.

To do this, for shorter rounds, before working instructions from ★, work Rounds 6-10 of Selbbob Bobbles chart or written instructions (see Glossary on next page), then work from ★ onwards for 8 rounds of bobbles.

selbbob bobbles.

crown shaping.

key.

☐	Worked with Yarn A&B held together
■	Worked with Yarn B, with Yarn A held at back
☐	repeat
	knit
⑪	bobble
C	M1tog
╱	k2tog
☐	Work in Yarn B only for first instance

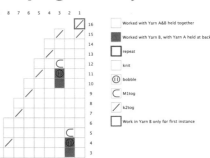

notions.

tapestry needle
stitch marker

glossary.

splitA&B

Using Yarn A&B held together, knit into the Yarn A and Yarn B sections of next stitch individually, as if they were 2 separate stitches. 1-st increase.

SELBBOB BOBBLES

(worked in the round over multiple of 10 sts)

Round 1 (bobble prep): [K6A&B, k1B, k3A&B] to end.
Round 2 (bobble): [K6A&B, bobB, k3A&B] to end.
Round 3 (catch): [K6A&B, M1tog, k3A&B] to end.
Rounds 4–5: Knit with A&B held together.
Round 6 (staggered prep): [K1A&B, k1B, k8A&B] to end.
Round 7 (staggered bobble): [K1A&B, bobB, k8A&B] to end.
Round 8 (staggered catch): [K1A&B, M1tog, k8A&B] to end.
Rounds 9–10: Knit with A&B held together.

BOBBLE (abbreviated to bob)

Kfb5 to make 5 sts out of 1 st; into the single-colour st from the preparatory round, kfb5 by working ktbl, kfb, kfb into the single-colour st. Turn work, p5, turn work, k5, turn work, p5, turn work, sl2tog kwise, k3tog, psso.

Note: The strand of the second yarn colour across the back helps to resolve one of the tricky bobble issues: the closing of the gap that forms between bobble and rest of knit. Give the second colour yarn (that floats across the back) an extra little tug to help this along, before continuing in yarn A&B held together.

If you fancy acquiring or practising backwards-knitting skills, they are eminently useful for knitting bobbles, as they mean you can work them without turning your work for each tiny row. You can find a nice, clear tutorial from Wendy Peterson of YarnSub at www.yarnsub.com/articles/techniques/knitting-backwards

MAKE 1, KNIT 2 TOGETHER (abbreviated to M1tog)

With a freshly knitted st on your right needle and the st from top of bobble (worked in previous round) still on your left needle, make 1 left-leaning st by lifting the horizontal strand of bobble-coloured yarn (leading to the bobble) from the round below and twisting it to form a loop. Place this loop on your left needle. Insert right needle into the bobble top st and the loop at once and knit them together as 1 st using Yarn A&B held together.

Note: Think of M1tog as a sort of M1L or M1R, where you don't knit into the new loop, but instead knit the loop together with the following st as if it were a k2tog. This will help to close the gap that otherwise often appears when a bobble is formed. No sts are increased or decreased, so your st count should remain the same.

pattern begins.

Cast-on note: Corrugated ribbing gives fabric a very distinct WS owing to the floats. Unlike ribbing worked in a single colour (which lies flat), the colourwork gives corrugated ribbing a tendency to curl up on the RS. One of the ways to minimise this is to work your stretchy cast-on a little tighter than you would normally. Obviously you need to ensure you don't go so tight it affects the stretch of the Brim so the hat doesn't fit well.

Using Yarn B, smaller needles and the long-tail method, cast on 132 (140, 148) sts, making sure the cast-on has enough stretch. Join in the round being careful not to twist.

corrugated rib brim.

Rib Set-up Round (Yarn B only): [K3, p1] to end.

This Rib Set-up Round sets your rib placement.

Note: The single 'tooth' of rib in Yarn B at the start of the Colour Set-up Round you are about to work is for the fun of it, because it's possible to switch out the colour of the rib at random in this way, but it's also a bit of a joke: a handmade, word- and logo-free reference to where companies often attach a 'tasteful' brand label. Placing it at the start of the round is both for ease of pattern writing and reading, and for the fun of having it be your marker for the beginning of each new round of rib.

Colour Set-up Round (Yarn A&B):

K3B, p1B, [k3A, p1B] to end.

Note: As you work the Corrugated Rib Brim, you may wish to work inside out if you are inclined to pulling your floats too tight. By seeing them as you work, it is easier to focus on keeping your tension even. For a lengthier insight into floats, see the Floats section of Working Marlisle on page 24.

The Colour Set-up Round sets your rib and colour placement. Work in rib as set by the Colour Set-up Round for a further 13 (15, 17) rounds until Brim measures 4 (4.5, 5)cm/1¼ (1½, 1¾)" from cast-on. Corrugated Rib Brim is now complete.

body.

Change to larger needles and PM at BOR (if not already using one).
Next Round: Knit with A&B held together.

Size S ONLY (dec): With A&B held together: K9, k2tog, k64, k2tog, knit to end. (2 sts dec) *130 sts*
Size M ONLY: Knit with A&B held together.
Size L ONLY (inc): With A&B held together: K9, splitA&B, k74, splitA&B, knit to end. (2 sts inc) *150 sts*

all sizes again.

Next Round: Knit with A&B held together.

Note: As you knit the bobbles, when and where the mood strikes, you can knit a single one in Yarn A instead of Yarn B. This could be in line with the single tooth of Yarn B in the Rib, the one on the very top or somewhere else entirely. Alternatively, work multiple bobbles in Yarn A. Prepare for it/them by working the single colour st in the Bobble Prep Round in the correct colour. When working a size L, beware that you don't knit too many, or you may need a second ball of Yarn A to finish the hat. The size L sample pictured with 5 bobbles of Yarn A had 3m/3¼ yds left.

★Work Rows 1-10 of Selbbob Bobbles chart or written instructions (see Glossary).
★★Repeat Rows 1-10 (boxed repeat) twice more, then repeat Rounds 1-3 (Rows 11-13 of Selbbob Bobbles chart) once more. You should have 7 rounds of bobbles in total and work should measure 16 (16.5, 17)cm/6¼ (6½, 6¾)" from cast-on.

Note: This hat will look big as you make it, because it is worked straight for a good distance before being decreased quickly to create a slightly gathered effect at the top, to ensure a slouchy fit.

crown shaping decreases.
Work from following written instructions or Selbbob Crown chart. You will decrease by 13 (14, 15) sts each decrease round to end.
Round 1 (dec): [K8A&B, k2togA&B] to end. *117 (126, 135) sts*
Round 2: Knit with A&B held together.
Round 3 (bobble prep): [K1A&B, k1B, k7A&B] to end.
Round 4 (bobble and dec): [K1A&B, bobB, k5A&B, k2togA&B] to end. *104 (112, 120) sts*
Round 5 (catch): [K1A&B, M1tog, k6A&B] to end.
Round 6: Knit with A&B held together.
Round 7 (dec): [K6A&B, k2togA&B] to end. *91 (98, 105) sts*
Round 8: Knit with A&B held together.
Round 9 (dec): [K5A&B, k2togA&B] to end. *78 (84, 90) sts*
Round 10 (bobble prep): [K2A&B, k1B, k3A&B] to end.

Note: This last bobble doesn't extend up from the same place, but is skewed to make it central with the right-leaning decreases of the crown. It is also placed 6 rounds after the previous bobble, rather than the usual 4 rounds. Again, this makes more sense visually.

Round 11 (bobble and dec): [K2A&B, bobB, k1A&B, k2togA&B] to end. *65 (70, 75) sts*
Round 12 (catch): [K2A&B, M1tog, k2A&B] to end.
Round 13 (dec): [K3A&B, k2togA&B] to end. *52 (56, 60) sts*
Round 14: Knit with A&B held together.
Round 15 (dec): K2togA&B to end. *26 (28, 30) sts*
Round 16 (bobble prep and dec): K2togB, [k2togA&B] to end. *13 (14, 15) sts*

special finishing instructions.
Make a bobble in the prepared Yarn B st using Yarn B, then break Yarn B, pulling end through final bobble st. Break Yarn A and use end to thread through and tightly secure all 12 (13, 14) Yarn A&B sts, leaving bobble on RS of hat. Sew bobble into place. Weave in all remaining ends. Give it a good soak in your favourite wool-friendly detergent. Rinse, then squeeze out excess water, wrapping in a towel to get out even more moisture. Do not wring. To block, allow to dry over a balloon inflated to a little smaller than head size.

Both quilters and tile-setters will be especially familiar with the pattern in the yoke of this sweater. Knitters less so, because they would ordinarily have had to engage in the oft-spurned act of using three colours in a round to achieve this configuration. Thanks to Marlisle, it's possible with just two, as using them in combination provides the third shade required. Those who use needle and thread to piece shapes together, rather than a trowel and mortar, will know this pattern as Tumbling Blocks. It is made up of three diamonds in three different colours tessellated to create a hexagon with the appearance of a 3D square (that also looks like honeycomb from beehives). In the fabled visual language 'written' in quilts of the Underground Railroad (the secret community network that helped slaves in the USA escape to freedom) this pattern, which resembles boxes, was used to give the alert that conditions were right to pack up and go.

yarn pairing notes.

For me, places are inextricably bound with people. In that sense, people make places, so where I have a friend they become part of my appreciation of the geography. Picking yarns that reflect a place involves being realistic about what is most easily available there, but also who lives there. Inspired by the fact that this pattern appears in tiles and quilts, this yarn combination hails from Portugal (because of Rosa Pomar and the country's beautiful tiles) and Australia (we'll come to the reason why in a bit).

The undyed yarn comes from Rosa Pomar, without whose yarn this book would have felt incomplete. Viewed from afar, she is on a one-woman crusade to preserve Portuguese wool craft traditions via her shop, Retrosaria, in Lisbon. I say "viewed from afar" because I hope the woolly cause in Portugal has more champions: there's a lot of history there for one individual to be sole custodian of. She works closely with artisans, from shepherds to spinners (both hand and mechanised), to help find a new audience to support skills and equipment that might otherwise pass out of understanding. Of her growing range of Portuguese yarns — encompassing the finest laceweight to chunky — I have chosen Mé-Mé 20, a heavy, single-ply laceweight, named for the sound of the sheep it comes from (of which it smells richly). It was the first yarn Rosa sold, early in 2010, later unavailable for a few years, while the mill went through bankruptcy before being able to reopen. From sheep to yarn, it is entirely produced in the Serra da Estrela mountains, where it is traditionally used for the weaving of blankets and is an integral part of local culture, from the way of life of the shepherds to the DOP-designated Serra da Estrela cheese, which comes from the milk of the same sheep. The mountainous grazing grounds of the flocks of mostly Bordeliera and Churros Mondegueira are conjured up for the knitter by the odd bits of vegetation that have crept into the spin. Because these sheep are bred for their milk production rather than for meat or wool, they produce a short, fairly coarse fleece. This is a bonus byproduct, an added value rather than the end goal, but it always has been made use of because it is a player in a cycle of production. In this way it is a vital part of an eco-system and a good reminder that yarn like this shouldn't be ignored in our quest for the softest softie soft yarn. And, as a reward for us understanding how it is a part of the bigger picture, this yarn that is so 'rustic' during the knitting process blooms and softens with washing and wear.

And next you ask, but why Australia? What has that got to do with Tumbling Blocks?

Well, simply because it is there that I learned the basics of quilting from my friend Jo Dunsmuir. Alongside making beautifully simple quilts with just the right sort of wonk, Jo sews the Frankie & Ray dresses and shirts I can often be found wearing and she increasingly creates patterns for the DIY stitcher.

For a country that has so many sheep, you might imagine that sheep-to-shop yarns were ten-a-penny in Australia, to be found in every LYS and farmer's market. In fact, they are only slightly easier to come by than hens' teeth. A spanner in the works is the limited access to spinning mills for those who might rock up with fleeces from their own flock. Most small producers have to work with mills in nearby New Zealand. The limits placed on production by forces outside small producers' influence are an example of the sometimes impracticable desire for single-country-origin yarns. It is worth bearing in mind that both Melbourne and Sydney are closer to the New Zealand cities of Christchurch and Wellington than to Perth, their Australian compatriot.

The Australian market for yarn, whether domestic or imported, has long been dominated by the type of large brands that move production abroad to save costs, turning a blind eye to the infrastructures lost in those changes and unfazed by replacing them with processes and practices 'overseas' that we like to think wouldn't fly on our home turf (wherever our 'home turf' is in comparison to the 'overseas'). Much of the fleece from Australian flocks heads outside the national borders. But with an increasingly passionate audience for more natural and place-specific, traceable yarns, there is growing support for small brands such as Tarndie, White Gum Wool, Millpost and Wool Days as well as a keen market for hand-dyed yarns. If you are curious to know more, Georgie Nicolson of Tikki Knits keeps 'The Great Aussie Yarn' database at www.tikkiknits.com/the-great-aussie-yarn.html, which is a clear and generous resource for locals and yarn tourists alike. Indications are good that Australia will soon have a thriving scene — particularly remarkable in a country where huge swaths of it are so hot, there's little call for woolly jumpers.

For my Aussie-related yarn, I wanted to reflect a bit of both these realities. I turned to Hannah Ginn of Circus Tonic Handmade, who lives in Sydney. She and I have had many good conversations about yarn and dyeing, including her quest to find more local, sheepy bases. Her Circus Single is a super-soft and airy Merino. I have mostly shied away from Merino for this collection, because it is so familiar, such a simple shortcut to saying 'soft', that we often forget it is a breed. But to get it from

Australia, the country with which contemporary Merino is so strongly associated, well, there was a reason for it. Interestingly though, this one is raised and spun in Peru and reaches Hannah by way of Chester Wools in the UK (owned and run by Andy Robinson with Jeni Hewlett on hand for dye know-how). This collection of yarns is about acknowledging what we, as knitters and dyers, have and hold close at hand. A yarn like this is part of the truth: a reflection that, though there are growing numbers of us: as a global entity, knitters are a comparatively small market and hand-dyers an even more boutique crowd amongst us. We don't all live somewhere with a small rare-breed producer a ball of yarn's throw away. (And, at that, one who produces yarn in significant enough quantities to be able to make it available for others to dye.) But friendships also have an important role to play in navigating choices, wool has long been part of international trade and things could be far worse. To tie it all together, Hannah is also a quilter! To reflect the excitement of all of these connections and the shimmering nature of the marl sections in the sweater's yoke, the 'tumbling' of Tumbling Blocks morphed into Trembling, to become the name of this pattern.

For me, working these two specific yarns together is a treat for fingers and mind. One from a place with thousands of years of historical wool usage and the other with a comparatively scant two hundred years under her belt. There's so much richness in pondering ways to safeguard futures and preserve the history of complicated and woolly traditions while two very different yarns pass through your fingers at once. I like the idea that it's match-making these two very different characters who get to be paired into a sweater — their very different histories making for a more beautiful, shared future. One that encourages embracing all the possibilities with generosity.

construction and fit.

A loose-fitting, but not oversized, lightweight sweater with full-length sleeves, Trembling is knitted in the round from the top down. To keep you cosy and warm, the striking, densely knitted yoke gives extra warmth across the shoulders where it is usually welcome. Almost imperceptible increases and start-of-round transitions are hidden in the diamonds to make for uninterrupted geometric patterning. You'll also be hard-pressed to find the short rows that run across the back and front of the shoulders to shape the round neckline for a superior fit. The majority of short rows are carefully placed so you can work them on simple garter-stitch rounds using both yarns together, reducing the need to

do colourwork from the wrong side. To further reduce the amount of stitches you work from the wrong side, the usual crescent of short rows is flipped. You start with the longest short row close to the neckband (while the rounds contain fewer stitches). This means the shortest length short rows can be worked further down, when you have increased the rounds to include more stitches. The intense yoke is balanced out by a soothingly simple stocking-stitch body (worked straight) and sleeves (tapered at regular intervals) that are finished off by easy 2x2 ribbing to stop any chance of roll.

sizing.

XS (S, M, L, XL, XXL)
Designed to be worn with approx 10cm/4" positive ease around bust.

yarn.

Yarn A: Retrosaria Mé-Mé 20 (4ply/fingering (see note below); 100% wool from the Serra da Estrela region of Portugal; 167m/183yds per 50g/1¾oz)
Grey (2) x 6 (6, 7, 7, 8, 8)

Yarn B: Circus Tonic Handmade, Circus Single Ply (4ply/fingering; 100% Merino (machine washable); 366m/400yds per 100g/3½oz)
Emerald City or Mallard x 1 (This will be plenty for sizes XS, S, M and L. For sizes XL and XXL, it will be enough, but the allowance is less generous.)

It is important to chose two yarns with a striking colour contrast. They need to be different enough separately to create a clear third colour when used together, especially if you are using single-ply yarns, which have a tendency to blend together more than multi-ply yarn. Using two single-ply yarns has the benefit of reducing the bulk that results from using densely spun 4ply/fingering weight yarns intended for sturdy socks and mittens.

While Mé-Mé 20 is referred to as a laceweight elsewhere, it is best to consider it a light 4ply/fingering weight in terms of substitution. Using the specified yarn at the given stocking-stitch gauge will result in a loose stocking stitch; not so much as to be lacy, but not dense at all. This means you can substitute a slightly thicker yarn (which will give a slightly bulkier Yoke), but not a finer yarn. A true laceweight would certainly not fit the bill. Mé-Mé comes in three different weights, so make sure you are looking at the right one.

worn by...

Marilla in Grey (2) and Emerald City, size M, knitted by Anna Maltz and Pien Maltz-Klaar.
Adam in Grey (2) and Mallard, size M, knitted by Anna Maltz and Pien Maltz-Klaar.

gauge.

24 stitches x 36 rounds = 10cm x 10cm/4" x 4" over stocking stitch in Yarn A only on larger needle after blocking. (Main gauge) (For Body and Sleeves.)
26 stitches x 34 rounds = 10cm x 10cm/4" x 4" over Marlisle Trembling stitch pattern in Yarn A and B on larger needle after blocking. (For Yoke.)
24 stitches x 40 rounds = 10cm x 10cm/4" x 4" over 2x2 Ribbing in Yarn A on smaller needle after blocking.
(For Cuffs and Bottom Ribbing.)

needles.

3.5mm (US4) circular needle for Body and Yoke at least 80cm/32" long. If making sizes L, XL or XXL your stitches may fit more easily on a 100cm/40" needle.
3.5mm (US4) needles suitable for working small circumferences in the round for Sleeves and start of Yoke.
2.75mm (US2) needles for Bottom Ribbing at least 80cm/32" long. If making sizes L, XL or XXL your stitches may fit more easily on a 100cm/40" needle.
2.75mm (US2) needles suitable for working small circumferences in the round for Cuff and Neckband.

Always use a needle size that will result in the correct gauge after blocking.

Needle size note: Choosing your main (larger) needle size should be based on achieving the Yarn A-only stocking-stitch gauge. Only one needle size is suggested for the Yoke, Body and Sleeves. This will give you tighter colourwork and looser single-colour stocking stitch. Be prepared to play around with needle size, if this is not the case for you. You may need to use two slightly different-size needles: one for the Marlisle part of the Yoke and another for the stocking-stitch Yoke, Body and Sleeves, in addition to the needle size for working the ribbing.

notions.

tapestry needle
locking stitch marker
smooth waste yarn, 2 stitch holders or spare needles for putting Sleeve Top sts on hold

glossary.

CORRUGATED BROKEN RIB
(worked in the round over multiple of 5 sts)
Round 1: [K1B, k2A, k2B] to end.
Round 2: [P2A, k1A, k1B, p1B] to end.

2x2 RIB
(worked in the round over multiple of 4 sts)
Every round: [K1, p2, k1] to end.

schematic.

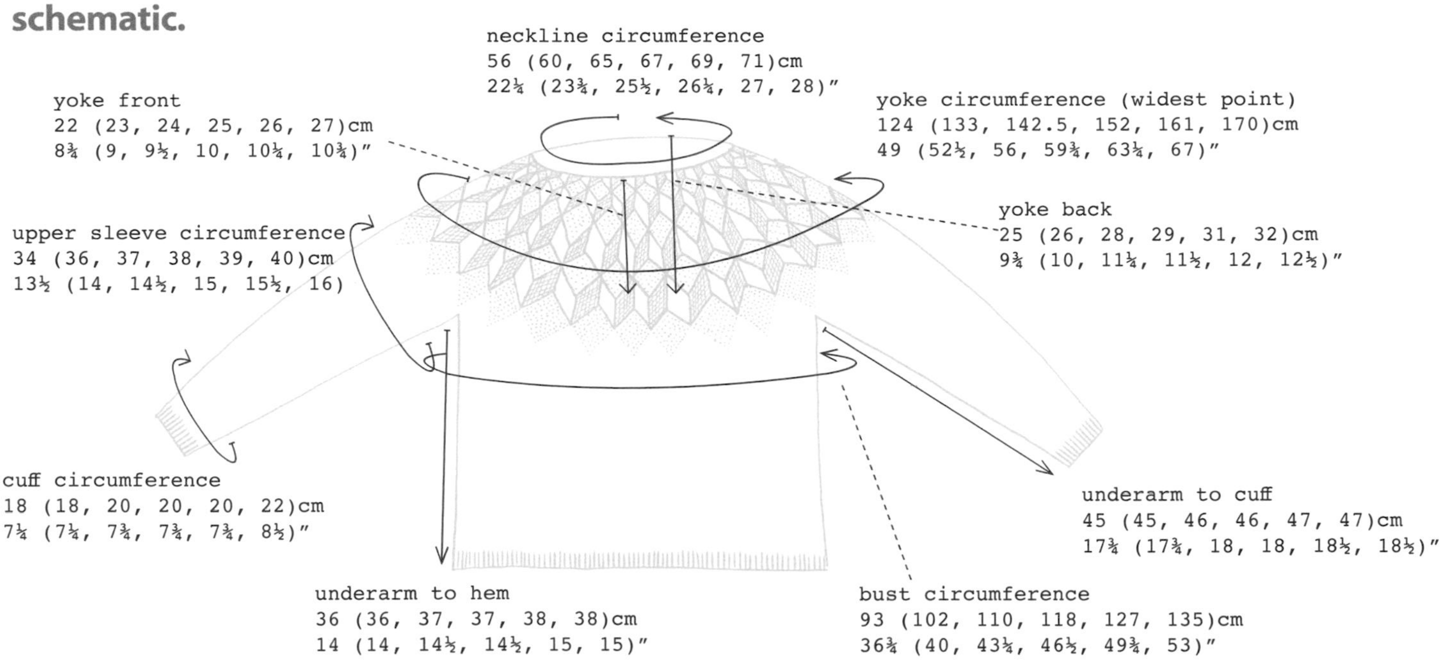
neckline circumference
56 (60, 65, 67, 69, 71)cm
22¼ (23¾, 25½, 26¼, 27, 28)"
yoke front
22 (23, 24, 25, 26, 27)cm
8¾ (9, 9½, 10, 10¼, 10¾)"
yoke circumference (widest point)
124 (133, 142.5, 152, 161, 170)cm
49 (52½, 56, 59¾, 63¼, 67)"
upper sleeve circumference
34 (36, 37, 38, 39, 40)cm
13½ (14, 14½, 15, 15½, 16)
yoke back
25 (26, 28, 29, 31, 32)cm
9¾ (10, 11¼, 11½, 12, 12½)"
cuff circumference
18 (18, 20, 20, 20, 22)cm
7¼ (7¼, 7¾, 7¾, 7¾, 8½)"
underarm to cuff
45 (45, 46, 46, 47, 47)cm
17¾ (17¾, 18, 18, 18½, 18½)"
underarm to hem
36 (36, 37, 37, 38, 38)cm
14 (14, 14½, 14½, 15, 15)"
bust circumference
93 (102, 110, 118, 127, 135)cm
36¾ (40, 43¼, 46½, 49¾, 53)"

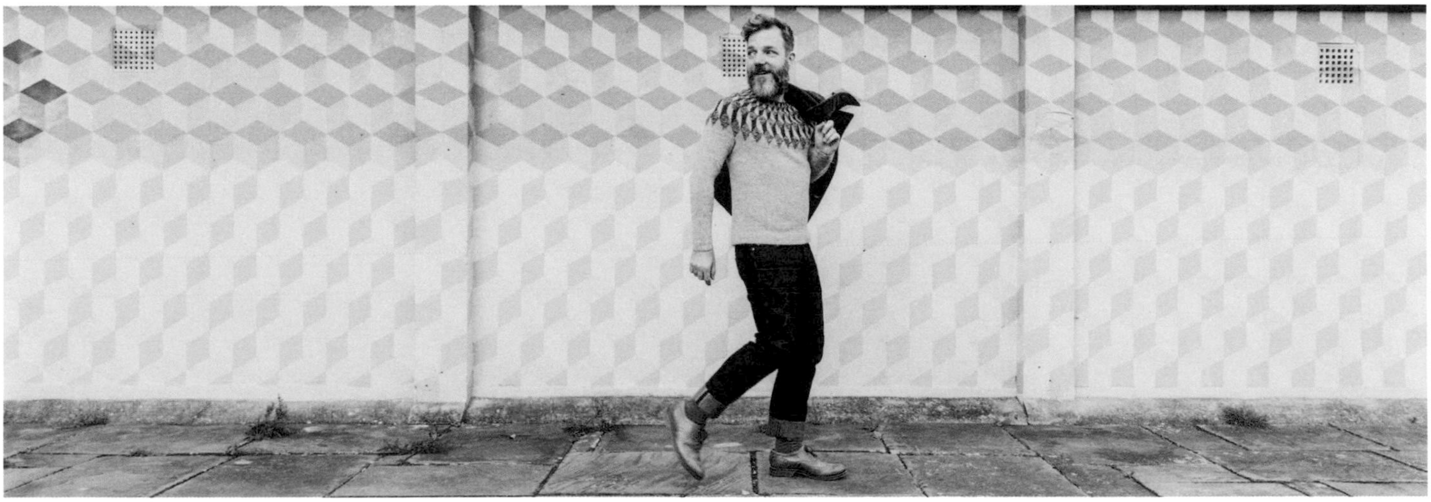

adapting trembling.

Personalising body shape: If you would like to personalise the pattern by adding body-shaping, perhaps to make it A-line or hourglass, or if you would like to make it longer/shorter, you should work the Sleeves first, rather than the Body, as this will allow you to get a truer idea of how the Body will fit once the sweater is complete. See the See Adapting Midstream (page 94) for more elaborate suggestions, remembering that you will be working from the top-down instead, in just one colour and will need to end with a st count that can be divided by 4 to have the ribbing work.

Adapting Sleeve length: The Sleeves are designed to be full length. Working from the top down, the paired decreases on the inside arm will bring you to exactly where you need to work the ribbed Cuff. You may wish to tweak the length of your Sleeves to fit your body or need to do so to accommodate for your round gauge.

For longer Sleeves (or to adjust for shorter round gauge): You can choose to work the Cuff a few rounds longer. For a greater difference, work some extra rounds before the Cuff. Add the extra rounds straight after all paired decreases are complete until Sleeve is 4cm/1½" short of desired length. Work Cuff.

For shorter Sleeves (or to accommodate for a longer round gauge): Instead of working 6 (6, 6, 5, 5, 5) rounds between Sleeve Decrease Rounds, work only 5 (5, 5, 4, 4, 4). When you have finished all decreases, work straight (if needed) until Sleeve is 4cm/1½" short of desired length. Work Cuff. You can also work 2, 4 or 6 fewer paired decreases to have significantly shorter Sleeves. Make sure that your total number of sts is divisible by 4 before starting on the Cuff.

key.

- Worked with Yarn B only, with Yarn A held at back
- Worked with Yarn A only, with Yarn B held at back
- Worked with Yarn A&B held together
- Rib Repeat - work 3 times
- knit
- • purl
- psplitA&B
- no stitch
- kfb
- Move BOR marker behind last st of Round 51 and count this as the first worked st of Round 52. This is now your BOR marker
- short row cycle worked on this round

pattern begins.

yoke.

The Yoke is worked from the Neckband down to where you divide for Body and Sleeves, with increases spread evenly around the circumference. Short rows are worked across the back half of the Yoke to improve the fit and give the neckline a slight scoop at the front. As you work the Marlisle Yoke, don't be alarmed by how sculptural it looks. This should come from the natural effect of the interaction between the held-double 'marl' and single 'isle' sections, not from your floats being too tight (though it is worth checking if they are). The ruching will mostly block out during the finishing process, unless you want to encourage it to stay.

Using Yarn B, larger needle and the long-tail method, cast on 135 (145, 155, 160, 165, 170) sts. Change to smaller needle. Join in the round being careful not to twist. PM to mark BOR. The BOR falls to the left front of neckline.

TREMBLING YOKE CHART
The Marlisle part of the Yoke is worked according to the Trembling Yoke chart for your chosen size and accompanying written instructions.

important note.
If working Yoke for sizes XS, S, M or L, you may spot that some row numbers appear to be missing from the chart. This is intentional, to keep the written instructions for the short rows as simple as possible. Do not substitute anything when you come to a 'missing' row — go straight to the next one on the chart. These are:

Size XS
Rows 13, 30, 31, 54 and 55. Rows 1, 2 and 12 are present, but you will not work them. You will work 75 rounds according to the chart, 6 of which are 3 repeats of Rib 1-2.

Size S
Rows 13, 30, 31, 54 and 55. You will work 78 rounds according to the chart, 6 of which are 3 repeats of Rib 1-2.

Sizes M & L
Rows 13, 31, and 55. You will work 80 rounds according to the chart, 6 of which are 3 repeats of Rib 1-2.

Sizes XL & XXL
There are no missing rows on the chart. You will work 83 rounds according to the chart, 6 of which are 3 repeats of Rib 1-2.

neckband.
Colour Dominance note: In regards to colour dominance, you will get better results if you pick a position to hold each yarn in and then stick with that for the duration of the neckband. For example, if you are used to two-handed colourwork, holding Yarn A in your right hand (to throw) and Yarn B in your left hand (to pick), will keep colour dominance issues in check and also make

working the rib a little more straightforward as you will be working the majority of the purl sts with your right hand (or reverse that if you find it easier to purl with your left hand). Later in the Yoke, where you are working stretches of Yarn A, Yarn B and Yarn A&B together in the same round, it will be hard to maintain these set positions. On the rounds where you work Yarn A and Yarn B as standard stranded colourwork, stick with the yarn-holding positions you establish for the Neckband. Write yourself a note if you are likely to forget.

Work 3 repeats (6 rounds) of Corrugated Broken Rib (see Glossary or Rib 1-2 on chart).

Change to larger needle.

short rows and increases.
Work short rows on the rounds indicated on chart and described in the written instructions below to raise the back and shape the neckline for a superior fit. Where you work the short rows, you will work all 3 partial rows that form the short row cycle in the st pattern as set by the row of the chart you are working the short row on. You do not progress to working from the next chart row until you have finished the backwards and forwards of the short row cycle that brings you back to the BOR. Work the short rows so that the stitches stacked on top maintain the stocking stitch and garter on the RS in the same yarn colours/combinations. You will need to work the pattern from the WS after the first w&t until you w&t again. When working the WS, you will need to work the single yarn sts as purls so that the stocking stitch is maintained on the RS and have the floats of the other yarn facing you, so they are on the WS and remain hidden on the RS.

Increase rounds should be worked according to the Trembling Yoke chart. You can find details of the number of sts to increase by and the resulting total number of sts in the written instructions.

Round 5 (short row) (all sizes):
K94 (104, 109, 109, 114, 114)A&B, w&t round following st, on WS k95 (105, 110, 110, 115, 115)A&B to 1 st past marker, w&t round following st, knit A&B to end of round, working wrap with the wrapped st as you pass it.

Note: On this first short row, the WS short row will take you back to 1 st before the BOR. This is correct, as later on, at the end of Round 51, you will be moving the BOR 1 st back. But don't worry about it for now! On the next charted round, remember to work the remaining wrap with the wrapped st as you pass it. Do this on all future rounds after a short-row cycle, whenever you encounter an unworked wrapped st.

Round 6 (inc): Work Row 6 of chart.
(27 (29, 31, 32, 33, 34) sts inc) *162 (174, 186, 192, 198, 204) sts*

Round 12 (short row) (sizes XL and XXL ONLY): Work Row 12 of chart for - (-, -, -, 134, 134) sts, w&t round following st, still working from Row 12, but on WS with floats on WS, work - (-, -, -, 132, 132) sts in pattern as set, w&t round following st, work Row 12 as set to end, working wrap with the wrapped st as you pass it.

Round 14 (inc): Work Row 14 of chart.
(27 (29, 31, 32, 33, 34) sts inc) *189 (203, 217, 224, 231, 238) sts*

Round 20 (short row) (all sizes):
K129 (139, 150, 150, 153, 153)A&B, w&t round following st, on WS k126 (133, 147, 147, 147, 147)A&B, w&t round following st, knit A&B to end of round, working wrap with the wrapped st as you pass it.

Round 21 (inc): Work Row 21 of chart.
(27 (29, 31, 32, 33, 34) sts inc) *216 (232, 248, 256, 264, 272) sts*

Round 29 (short row) (sizes M and L ONLY): Work Row 29 of chart for - (-, 167, 167, -, -) sts, w&t round following st, still working from Row 29, but on WS with floats on WS, work - (-, 160, 160, -, -) sts in pattern as set, w&t round following st, work Row 29 as set to end, working wrap with the wrapped st as you pass it.

Round 29 (short row) (sizes XL and XXL ONLY): Work Row 29 of chart for - (-, -, -, 171, 171) sts, w&t round following st, still working from Row 29, but on WS with floats on WS, work - (-, -, -, 160, 160) sts in pattern as set, w&t round following st, work Row 29 as set to end, working wrap with the wrapped st as you pass it.

Round 31 (short row) (sizes XL and XXL ONLY): Work Row 31 of chart for - (-, -, -, 167, 167) sts, w&t round following st, still working from Row 31, but on WS with floats on WS, work - (-, -, -, 152, 152) sts in pattern as set, w&t round following st, work Row 31 as set to end, working wrap with the wrapped st as you pass it.

Round 32 (inc): Work Row 32 of chart.
(27 (29, 31, 32, 33, 34) sts inc) *243 (261, 279, 288, 297, 306) sts*

Round 40 (short row) (all sizes):
K157 (170, 184, 184, 184, 184)A&B, w&t round following st, on WS, k143 (153, 171, 171, 162, 162)A&B to make a garter ridge on RS, w&t round following st, knit A&B to end of round, working wrap with the wrapped st as you pass it.

Round 41 (inc): Work Row 41 of chart.
(27 (29, 31, 32, 33, 34) sts inc) *270 (290, 310, 320, 330, 340) sts*

Round 51 (short row) (sizes M, L, XL and XXL ONLY):
Work Row 51 of chart for - (-, 199, 199, 199, 199) sts, w&t round following st, still working from Row 51, but on WS with floats on WS, work - (-, 180, 180, 170, 170) sts in pattern as set, w&t round following st, work Row 51 as set to end, working wrap with the wrapped st as you pass it.

marker realignment.

Now move marker back 1 st so that the last st of Round 51 (k1B) becomes the first st of Round 52 and do not work this st again until the beginning of Round 53. This is your new BOR.

Round 53 (short row) (sizes M and L ONLY): Work Row 53 of chart for - (-, 195, 195, -, -) sts, w&t round following st, still working from Row 53, but on WS with floats on WS, work - (-, 170, 170, -, -) sts in pattern as set, w&t round following st, work Row 53 as set to end, working wrap with the wrapped st as you pass it.

Round 56 (inc): Work Row 56 of chart.
(27 (29, 31, 32, 33, 34) sts inc) *297 (319, 341, 352, 363, 374) sts*

Round 66 (short row) (all sizes):
K182 (198, 209, 209, 215, 215)A&B, w&t round following st, on WS k154 (165, 176, 176, 176, 176)A&B to make a garter ridge on RS, w&t round following st, knit A&B to end of round, working wrap with the wrapped st as you pass it.

Rounds 72-77: As you are knitting the long stretches of Yarn A stocking stitch between the Yarn A&B Marlisle diamonds, catch your Yarn B floats in a couple of places in each repeat, until you finish working from the chart. Make sure to vary where you catch them from round to round, to avoid them showing more on the RS.

END OF TREMBLING YOKE CHART
297 (319, 341, 352, 363, 374) sts

Break Yarn B.

The rest of the sweater will be worked with Yarn A only in stocking stitch in the round, until you reach the Cuffs and Bottom Ribbing, which are worked in 2x2 Rib.

Next Round (partial round): K148 (164, 174, 177, 185, 187). Move marker from the Left Front to the end of Back, where your Right Sleeve Top will now start. Round starts here.

Adjustment Increase Round:
These increases (for fit) are carefully placed to help centre the neckline and patterning of the Yoke over the Body and Sleeves.

Sizes XS, S and M ONLY (inc): K253 (270, 288, -, -, -), M1R, knit to end. (1 st inc) *298 (320, 342, -, -, -) sts*

Size L only: *K22, M1R, k20, M1R, k22, [k22, M1R] x 2, k24, [M1R, k22] x 2,* repeat from * to * once more. (12 sts inc). *364 sts*

Size XL only: *[K13, M1R] x 2, k12, [M1R, k13] x 2,*k14, [M1R, k15] x 6, M1R, k14, repeat from * to * once more, [k13, M1R] x 8, k13. (23 sts inc) *386 sts*

Size XXL only: [K11, M1R] to end. (34 sts inc) *408 sts*

all sizes again.
298 (320, 342, 364, 386, 408) sts

Knit 0 (0, 2, 2, 5, 9) round/s straight.

body.
The Body (and Sleeves) extends down from the Yoke so that the charted patterning on the Yoke is centred in the middle of the neckline (between the short rows) and mirrored to both sides where the Sleeves start.

PUTTING SLEEVE TOPS ON HOLD AND ADDING UNDERARM STS
★Slide next 60 (62, 64, 66, 68, 70) sts on to a length of smooth waste yarn on hold for Sleeve Top (to be worked later). Using the backwards-loop method, cast on 23 (24, 25, 26, 27, 28) sts to create the Underarm that spans the gap between Back and Front.★
Knit across 89 (98, 107, 116, 125, 134) sts. Repeat from ★ to ★ once more. Knit to end. *224 (244, 264, 284, 304, 324) sts*

Note: See Adapting Trembling (page 135), for tips on personalising the Body shape.

Work straight for 115 (115, 119, 119, 122, 122) rounds.
After blocking, Body should measure 32 (32, 33, 33, 34, 34)cm/ 12½ (12½, 13, 13, 13¼, 13¼)" from Underarm at this stage.

bottom ribbing.
Change to smaller needles.
Work 14 rounds of 2x2 rib (see Glossary) till Bottom Ribbing measures 4cm/1½".

Cast off in rib as set, making sure to allow sufficient stretch in the cast-off. It may help to change to a larger needle size.

sleeves.
Both Sleeves are worked alike from the held Sleeve Top sts on the Yoke from the shoulder down to the Cuff in stocking stitch with decreases worked in pairs along a 'seam' under the arm. When you reach the Cuff, it will be worked in 2x2 Rib. See Adapting Trembling (page 135) for suggestions on adapting Sleeve length.

Note: When continuing from the Yoke into the separate Body and Sleeves, it's inevitable that a hole and/or elongated sts will form at the edges of the Sleeve where the Underarm sts meet the Sleeve Top sts between Yoke and Body. This can partly be remedied by easing the extra slack out across the surrounding sts. At one side you will have an end (from starting the Sleeve) that, at the same time as you weave it in, you can use to sew closed any holes that appeared. There will not be an end to use on the other side. One way to minimise this hole is to pick up 2 or 3 extra sts around the transition from Sleeve Top to Underarm sts, then in the next round, decrease these sts back down to the official st count you need to continue with the Sleeve. Sizes XS, M and XL already require you pick up an extra st in relation to the number you need to work the Sleeve (this is so that you pick up 1 st for every st you cast on for the Body Underarm). This extra st is decreased in the following round. You can choose to pick up a couple more to decrease in the following round for these and the other sizes. If you decrease them where the hole usually forms, you can gather any gap together by using k2tog and/or ssk, whichever blends in best. The required st to decrease for sizes XS, M and XL is not placed at the edge to join the Sleeve Top sts to the Underarm sts, but in the centre of the Underarm, to be in line with the Sleeve decreases,

in case you do not want to work the decreases at the edge. If you want to close a gap, move it to the edge and make sure that your round still starts in the centre of the Underarm.

PREPARE SLEEVE TOP STS FOR ACTION

With larger needles and RS facing, working from right to left, pick up and knit 23 (24, 25, 26, 27, 28) sts from the backwards-loop Underarm cast-on edge. Knit across 60 (62, 64, 66, 68, 70) Sleeve Top sts. *83 (86, 89, 92, 95, 98) sts*

Next Round (partial): K10 (12, 11, 13, 12, 14), k2tog 1 (0, 1, 0, 1, 0) time, PM to mark BOR. *82 (86, 88, 92, 94, 98) sts* Round now starts here for remainder of Sleeve.

Work straight in stocking stitch for 15 (1, 11, 19, 17, 17) rounds.

**Sleeve Decrease Round:

K1, ssk, knit till 3 sts remain, k2tog, k1. (2 sts dec) Work straight for 6 (6, 6, 5, 5, 5) rounds.**

Repeat from ** to ** a further 18 (20, 19, 21, 22, 22) times for a total of 19 (21, 20, 22, 23, 23) pairs of decreases. *44 (44, 48, 48, 48, 52) sts*

Note: At the start of a Sleeve, you may want to experiment with making a bundle of the Body and Yoke (and later second Sleeve) by tying them together with an elastic band or piece of string, so you don't have a giant flappy thing to rotate every time you knit a Sleeve round. Once the Sleeve is longer, it's easier to let it twist up as you knit and then untwist occasionally.

cuff.
Change to smaller needles.
Repeating [k1, p2, k1], work 14 rounds of 2x2 rib till Cuff measures 4cm/1½".

Cast off in rib as set, making sure to allow sufficient stretch in the cast-off. It may help to change to a larger needle size.

special finishing instructions.
Once all ends are woven in and sweater has been soaked and squeezed dry, ease into shape, allowing to dry flat with the Front RS facing (remembering that the back neckline should be higher than the front because of the short rows). Pay attention as, when working a single-ply yarn alone, as in the Sleeves and Body, the fabric will likely have a distinct bias twist that comes from the spin of the yarn. Straighten the rounds as best you can during the blocking process, so that sts run straight up to the centre of the neckline and to the Underarms on each side of the Body. On the Sleeves, make sure the line of decreases runs straight under the arm, rather than in a spiral. Be careful to not stretch out the ribbing on Cuff and Bottom edge, to allow it to retain as much natural elasticity as possible once dry. See General Finishing Instructions on page 142 for additional guidance.

Casting off the final stitch of a project is just the first step of your knit being done. I suggest you finish as outlined below. When more pattern-specific advice is called for, refer to the Special Finishing Instructions at the end of each pattern.

secure. check. weave.

OK, here we go. Make sure all stitches are secured — this mostly means the ones at the end of a cast-off, but it's also a good moment to do an all-over check to see if you've dropped a stitch somewhere. Weave in all ends. Don't snip them off too close to the fabric, or they are likely to pop out the other side as soon as you wash and wear your knit.

water or hot, wet air.

I'm a full-immersion wet-blocker, so that's what you'll read about here. The woolly wools I gravitate to and Marlisle (like other forms of stranded colourwork) benefit from a good soak. Steam-blocking is also an option, but not one I use, for personal reasons — I try to keep the ironing I do to a minimum, so I save those odd occasions for the likes of lovely dresses sewn from Marilla Walker or Frankie & Ray patterns. Irons are hot — and best used with additional caution around silk and synthetics, including bamboo-based viscose. My iron spits out bits of calcified gunk, because I live in a hard-water area and don't like to treat it to bottled water. And there's stuff I want to wash out of my knit — from the sheep, the spinning process and while it's a WIP.

fill and dunk.

Fill a vessel (sink, bowl, bucket or tub), big enough to submerge the whole item in, with cold water (or lukewarm, if your hands will freeze) and a small amount of your favourite wool-friendly detergent evenly dispersed in it. Shampoo works in a pickle. On occasion, hair conditioner can be nice to add, if your wool needs a little softening aid. Place your knit in the water and help the air out, so it's fully submerged. The idea is just to leave it in the water, not to agitate it, as this could encourage felting, or misshaping while the fibres are more sensitive.

watch out for bleeding.

Be careful when soaking two colours together — colour fastness is a factor to consider, especially (not exclusively), when using hand-dyed yarn. Bleeding dye can be terrible for any colourwork project. A splash of transparent and pale-coloured vinegar (ie. not red-wine vinegar!!!) in the water can help keep colours in place. Not too much, or you'll end up smelling like salad-dressing or a chip shop.

If you are confident of the colours (because your swatch didn't run) or are using a combination of shades where a little muddling isn't a big deal (such as any dyed colour in combo with a deep, dark, natural, undyed brown), allow a soak of at least 30 minutes (just a quick dip to wet through, if you're not). If something distracts you, there's no need to worry if it ends up being in there for a few hours. This process will help even out the inevitable nobbles and bobbles of fluctuations in tension that come with knitting colourwork (especially with texture).

rinse.

Upscale wool washes advertise their no-need-to-rinse nature, which is highly beneficial when using yarns so soft they have a tendency to pill just from being looked at. More sturdy, natural yarns will benefit from being rinsed — they are processed significantly less before making their way on to your needles and will contain more debris from the sheep's life and the spinning process. Just make sure that the water is the same temperature as the water you have been soaking it in — changes in temperature are another factor in encouraging felting.

squeeze.

Next, you want to remove as much water as you can by gently squeezing out the excess, without allowing the fabric to overly stretch while laden down with water. Never, ever wring out your knitting. Wrap it in a towel to get out even more moisture. Standing or sitting on it while it's rolled in a towel can help squish out extra moisture. Just make sure to get up before you get a wet bum, if you plump for the sitting! Alternatively, if you want to engage in the risky activity of putting it in a spindrier or through your washing machine's spin-only cycle, make sure to knot it securely into a pillowcase first (to protect it) and confirm the settings BEFORE you press the on button. My mum trusts her washing machine so much that she puts handknitted jumpers through the whole wool cycle. I do not.

block.

To block, ease the knit into the measurements specified on the pattern's schematic and the size you followed. Though they are extra kit to acquire, using a blocking mat and wires, as well as lots of pins, can be highly beneficial to train your knit into smoothly drying to the dimensions you are after. In other words, the blocking process will make your knitted fabric look even better and help anchor your garment to the shape you want it to be, based on the measurements specified in the pattern (remember, accessories worn on the body are garments too).

Spread your knit out on an appropriately sized and shaped surface, tweaking it into place. Don't even think about putting it on a hanger! You want it to be fully supported. This generally means as flat as possible (unless it's a hat) — think bed, couch, ironing board, blocking mats, clean carpet, etc. Flat works for headgear too — as long as you don't have the fold exactly where the intended front will be. You can get creative, drying hats over

a balloon (inflated smaller than the size of your head) or an upturned bowl, or whatever else will give a nice smooth, rounded shape. A milliners block could work a treat here, if you have one. Gently ease the garment into shape and open out the pattern. Any areas that will benefit from retaining their natural stretch, such as ribbing, should not be stretched out and should instead be left to dry as condensed as possible.

Check to make sure everything is straight that needs to be straight, or curved, if that's what's called for. This includes the patterning of the stitches — if you're using pins, you can use them in the middle too, not just on the outside edges, if this will help train the shapes you want (be that pointy triangles or straight lines, such as a Decorative Seam — DS). Unless you are great at eyeballing, rulers and tape measures are indispensable tools for checking things are straight and the same length or shape. For those of us with symmetrical bodies, we are looking for a pair of mitts or mittens to be the same size for both hands and our left sleeve and side of body the same length as the right.

be patient.

It's worth taking a good amount of time to block sweaters and cardigans really precisely and carefully, even if that means significantly upwards of an hour of crawling around on hands and knees or awkwardly reaching over a bed to do so. This will help the knit shine and honour the materials and time you have put in thus far. The joy of wool is that it doesn't need

(or benefit) from regular laundering, so consider this an investment of time spread across the year/s you won't ever need to wash this woolly again.

dry.

Step away from the knit. Different types, as well as weights, of yarn take more or less time to dry. Dense areas of Marlisle can take their sweet time. It will also depend on the climate and season you are in, and how much ventilation there is. Be patient and wait until it is totally dry before removing all the pins.

wear.

Slip it on and feel chuffed! You should feel very proud of what you have made. Accept compliments graciously. There's no need to point out any mistake/s only you know about. No one else will notice them — they are focused on admiring the wonder of your handiwork.

For further discussions of blocking and finishing, refer to the instructions for swatching in The Fabric chapter, page 22.

avoiding frustrations.

speed.

Unlike a meal required on the table to satisfy rumbling bellies, these knitting recipes are not billed as 'quick'. At the same time, because they use two yarns held together, this does have the effect of speeding things up in comparison to using one of the same yarns singly. There's never an easy answer! When it comes to knitting, I like to remember my brother-in-law's approach to cooking. He feels immensely proud that he can complete one of Jamie Oliver's 30-minute recipes in an hour. These patterns do not come with an expected or projected timeframe. They are intended to be slow, considered and satisfying projects, where the process is part of the joy. Extra satisfaction is added by working them with invigorating materials that help nourish the community we love, made by people who feel responsible for preserving the environment, skills and industry. We know that the planet is already immensely full of stuff and it's worth taking our time over what we choose to add to it. The hope is that the resulting garments will be worn with pleasure for many years to come, and then mended to extend their life further, perhaps into someone else's life.

twisting yarns.

The two yarns will inevitably twist together while you are working, especially during rounds involving both knit and purl stitches. Don't worry! When you next reach a stretch of marled stitches (any long steek sections work extra well for this), simply push the twisted section close to your needles and work the Yarn A&B stitches with the twisty stretch of yarn. You can also untwist the yarn as you knit single-colour stitches, by being conscious of picking it up from the side of the twist that will help unwind it.

If you do need to untwist, popping your yarns in a zip-lock bag and sealing it tight around the yarn strand(s) sticking out, or putting an elastic band around each ball of yarn, will prevent them undoing further while you untangle them. Sometimes you can just hold the project up by the yarn and let it spin around to untwist without needing to worry too much about the stitches jumping off the tips of the needles. If you are worried about this, try wrapping an elastic band around the needle tips to keep the stitches secured, or pop a cork on the ends.

The placement of the ball of yarn as you work from it tends to have some effect on how tangled you might get. You are more likely to get frustrating twists the closer the yarn is to you: keeping it in your lap or nearby on the table tends to exacerbate things, whereas having the yarn on the floor, by your side — perhaps even one on either side — seems to help. You may find that using the ball of yarn from the outside, rather than pulling the strand from the inside, also helps avoid twisting, but it will make the ball harder to work from if you plan to use it from in a project bag.

holes.

You're not alone in getting little holes when switching between using one yarn and two held together while shifting between knit and purl. A number of us have found that gaps can form, especially when transitioning from a single-colour knit stitch to a Yarn A&B purl stitch while trying not to pull your float too tight. I've found that it can help to work the purl stitch by wrapping the yarn the other way around than usual, to shorten the gap that creates the hole. Insert your needle into the stitch as usual, but instead of wrapping over and under the needle, wrap it under and then over to form a stitch. In the next round, you need to make sure to remember what you have done and insert the needle through the back loop to untwist the stitch as you work it. Certain patterns have been adapted to help minimise how these holes appear: particularly the Chevre Cowl (page 118), where the pattern has been tweaked to have a Yarn A&B knit stitch when transitioning from working Yarn A or B singly before what would otherwise be a Yarn A&B purl stitch.

vertical lines.

Is there a dropped stitch? No? Then what's that vertical line of gappy stitches? DPNs and magic loop are indispensable for working small circumferences in the round, but they do have a tendency to create a visible 'seam' involving the stitches where you transition between needles. It is very easy for these to become misshapen. To avoid this, you need to keep in mind a number of factors. Try to position the transitions away from where you will have floats, as keeping the tension consistent across floats is difficult when they fall at needle transitions. Equally, give a little thought to how you arrange stitches on the needles around increase and decrease shaping, as these don't need any additional encouragement to form lines. Avoid having needle transitions in feature areas of the project, such as right down the centre. Instead, try to conceal them somewhere less noticeable: down the sides, where folds will happen or under the arms. You can also regularly switch where the transitions between needles happen. With DPNs, this means knitting an extra stitch from the next needle. For magic loop, this means changing where your loops are. It's useful to remember that splitting the total number of stitches exactly in half across sides when

magic looping is just standard practice, and not essential. You can divide the stitches in a way that will help you keep track of what to do where, or where will best mask the pesky 'seam' that forms. For the most even results, use a circular needle that is the right length to easily accommodate the number of stitches you are working.

colour-pooling.

The standard advice on most hand-dyers' websites is to work from two balls of yarn, alternating them every couple of rows or rounds to throw off any colour-pooling that might occur. At a minimum, it's worth alternating rounds of the new and old balls as you transition between them to avoid any differences between them punctuating the overall effect. That said, none of the projects pictured in this book have been worked alternating throughout or even between new and old balls. This was a calculated risk, based on the fact that the marl sections add an element of blending in their own right and that solid and semi-solid, rather than variegated yarns, have been used. In only one out of the 25 samples made was there any reason to question having thrown caution to the wind like that. That's not a bad average, but you should choose for yourself, based on what your comfort levels are with the yarn you are using.

If you are convinced your dye lots are the same or are happy to embrace the transition of the differences between them, you can engage in the joyous activity of spit-splicing the new and old ends together. Or, if that makes your hygiene-conscious skin crawl at the prospect, join them in your preferred way. If you are working the Ess Shawl (page 84), Ruperto Scarf (page 110) or Shantay Cardigan (page 54), which all have steeks, you can either join by spit-splicing (if you are in the middle of a round) or, without joining the ends in any way, place the transition of ends in the centre of the steek section, in effect making that tiny section of the steek pre-cut.

frogging.

In the unfortunate event that you need to rip back some of what you've knitted, from experience, I highly recommend asking a buddy to help you. That way, each one of you can take charge of winding one of the colours of yarn, to help avoid a giant tangle or frustratingly slow going during what is already a frustrating task.

errata.

Much time and care has been taken to ensure these patterns are a pleasure to follow, and not just correct in the numbers. Regardless, there will still be hiccups that arise and for those please accept my sincere apologies in advance. The hope is that you will be able to work out your own satisfying solution or draw on the expertise of your knitting community. It is worth checking the relevant pattern page on Ravelry, or the errata page at www.annamaltz.com, to find out whether it is already a known issue. If you believe you have found a snafu that would benefit other knitters by being explained and added to the errata, please get in contact with a conciliatory, friendly email to errata@annamaltz.com.

download the code.

If you activate your personal download code, any future digital updates to patterns will automatically be available to you in your Ravelry library. Your download code can be found on a sticker in the front of your book or in an email received when you ordered directly from www.annamaltz.com.

terminology.

The majority of the terminology and techniques used in this book are fairly standard. Only a couple of them are peculiar to Marlisle. Where special terms and abbreviations are used, explanations can be found in the Glossary section of each individual pattern or at the relevant point in the pattern instructions. These special ones and their abbreviations are outlined in more length below.

(yarn A&B).

All the patterns in this book are worked using two yarns, referred to for simplicity as A and B. Yarn A is always the natural, undyed colour and Yarn B is the dyed one. This means that regardless of which yarn you start using first in the pattern instructions, Yarn A will be the sheepy colour and Yarn B will be the rainbow colour. Worked together, Yarn A&B in effect become a third colour. Direction is given to work particular instructions using A or B or A&B.

decorative seams (DS).

Decorative seams are worked at the start of a round to mask where the jog between rounds would otherwise occur. When working patterns using garter stitch as a constant background, it's worth remembering that garter stitch, much like stripes, creates a jog when worked in the round. Rather than with stripes, where it is the transition between colours that creates a jog, garter stitch creates a 'seam' at the transition between a round of knit and a round of purl. Because you are working in the round, this isn't a sewn seam, but it is clearly visible. It is altogether natural and just-how-it-is when working lines as part of a spiral, but it isn't always the most aesthetically pleasing. With Marlisle, you can create an intentional, decorative seam that masks this transition. You can see these seams function most clearly in the Hozkwoz Hat (page 40), Kraai Mitts (page 30) and Midstream Sweater (page 94). A DS does not alter what the rounds of knit and purl do in order to form garter stitch, you are just interrupting their transition with a deliberate vertical line of knit stitches. In the main, pay attention to the tension of the floats behind the DS, such as in the Kraai Mitts. In the Selbbob Hat (page 124), however, the DS in the ribbing functions as a tag — it marks the start of the round and is a sly nod to where a brand label might go on a purchased hat — so it also works if it sticks out a little as a result of tight floats.

Beyond being decorative, a DS also becomes an inbuilt stitch and progress marker. They are a convenient guideline for when and where to work increases or decreases with regular shaping on the likes of sleeves and yokes, as you will find in the Midstream Sweater (page 94) and Kraai Mitts (page 30). They are also a convenient way to delineate different pattern zones, such as between the back and front on the Delftig Mittens (page 72). They create a distinct edge at the edges of the Ess Shawl (page 84) and Ruperto Scarf (page 110), but are hidden at the turned-in steek edge of the Shantay Cardigan (page 54).

split increases.

This is a single-stitch increase method particular to where two yarns have been held together to form a single stitch in the previous round. You work into the Yarn A and Yarn B sections of the next stitch individually, as if they were 2 separate stitches. Where decreases are stacked above each other, it is worth either intentionally varying (to be random) or being totally consistent with whether you knit into Yarn A or B first to avoid the chance of a visible pattern forming.

(splitA&B).

Using Yarn A&B held together, knit into the Yarn A and Yarn B sections of the next stitch individually, as if they were 2 separate stitches.

(psplitA&B).

The purl version of splitA&B. Using Yarn A&B held together, purl into the Yarn A and Yarn B sections of next stitch individually, as if they were 2 separate stitches.

rows and/or rounds.

For the most part, the patterns in this book are worked in the round. A round refers to a round of the knitting/work starting with the next stitch, stopping directly before working the first stitch again once you have worked all the stitches as directed. Keep an eye out for where 'row' is written. 'Row' is used for a chart row (as it is flat) or for those very occasional rows to be worked in the structure of the knit: these are generally at the very start of a pattern to coincide with the suggested cast-on method, or as a short row in the sweaters and cardigan.

Patterns are given with round counts as standard and sometimes with required length too. If you are taking measurements while working on a project, say to check the length of body or sleeves, you should remember that the specified lengths are based on the blocked measurements.

reading charts.

Each row of a chart for circular knits should be read from right to left, in the direction you work the stitches. As all of the patterns in this book are worked in the round, you will find the round numbers listed on the right-hand side of the chart, as an indication of where you start your round and the direction in which you work your stitches. (For patterns worked flat, you would expect to find alternate row numbers listed to the right and left sides of the chart, to indicate on which side you should be starting

that row.) If there is a boxed repeat on the chart, you should repeat only the stitches within the box as directed. Generally, you should work the stitches in the column before the boxed repeat once as you work towards the boxed repeat, then work the stitches within the box, repeating them as directed or to the end of the round. If there are stitches after the boxed repeat, to the left-hand side of the chart, these should be worked at the end of the round or as directed.

Some instructions about how to work the chart are given in written form only, not as notations on the chart. These will include things such as how many times to work the boxed repeat for your size, where and how to work short rows and specific tips and tricks that will help you achieve a more satisfying knit. These cannot always be marked on or directly alongside the chart, but they can be found in the body of the written instructions.

The chart key shows you what the different symbols used in the chart mean, and how to work the stitches represented. If you are unfamiliar with an abbreviation used in the key, refer to the Abbreviations (page 150). The same symbol can appear as black or white, depending on the background chart colour. The colour of the symbol does not change the meaning of the symbol. The background colour of the chart box shows you which yarn/s to work the specified stitch in.

abbreviations.

**	Repeat as indicated.
[ ]	Repeat to end of round/row or as indicated.
”	Inch
A	Yarn A only – natural, undyed in all patterns.
A&B	Yarn A and B held together.
B	Yarn B only – indie hand-dyed in all patterns.
BOR	Beginning of round
CDD	Central Double Decrease. Double decrease with dominant central stitch; Slip 2 stitches together knitwise, knit next stitch, pass 2 slipped stitches over. 2-stitch decrease.
cm	Centimetre
dec	Decrease(d)
DPNs	Double-pointed needles
DS	Decorative Seam/s knitted in a single yarn.
g	Grams
inc	Increase(d)
k	Knit
kfb	Knit into front and back of next stitch for a single increase. 1-stitch increase.
kfb tbl	Knit into front and back of next stitch, entering first through the back loop, for a single increase where the stitch you are working was a yarn over in the previous round. 1 stitch increase.
ktbl	Knit into back of next stitch, entering first through the back loop.
kwise	Knitwise
k2tog	Knit 2 stitches together for a single right-leaning decrease by inserting right needle into 2 stitches at once and knitting them together as 1 stitch. 1-stitch decrease.
k3tog	Knit 3 stitches together for a double right-leaning decrease by inserting right needle into 3 stitches at once and knitting them together as 1 stitch. 2-stitch decrease.
k2togtbl	Knit 2 stitches together for a single left-leaning decrease by inserting right needle into back loops of 2 stitches at once and knitting them together as 1 stitch. 1-stitch decrease.

LLI	Left-leaning lifted increase. Work a stitch into the left shoulder of the stitch in the row below the stitch you have just worked. 1-stitch increased.
m	Metre
mm	Millimetre
MW/X/Y/Z	Marker W/X/Y/Z
M1L	Make 1 left-leaning stitch by lifting the horizontal strand from the round/row below between the freshly knitted stitch on your right needle and the next stitch on your left needle. Lift the strand with your left needle, inserting from front to back, then knit into the back of it with your right needle to create the stitch. 1-stitch increase.
M1R	Make 1 right-leaning stitch by lifting the horizontal strand from the round/row below between the freshly knitted stitch on your right needle and the next stitch on your left needle. Lift the strand with your left needle, inserting from back to front, then knit into it with your right needle to create the stitch. 1-stitch increase.
oz	Ounce
p	Purl
P1L	Make 1 left-leaning stitch by lifting the horizontal strand from the round/row below between the freshly knitted stitch on your right needle and the next stitch on your left needle. Lift the strand with your left needle, inserting from front to back, then purl into the back of it with your right needle to create the stitch. 1-stitch increase.
P1R	Make 1 right-leaning stitch by lifting the horizontal strand from the round/row below between the freshly knitted stitch on your right needle and the next stitch on your left needle. Lift the strand with your left needle, inserting from back to front, then purl into it with your right needle to create the stitch. 1-stitch increase.

p2tog	Purl 2 stitches together for a single right-leaning decrease by inserting right needle into 2 stitches at once and purling them together as 1 stitch. 1-stitch decrease.
p2togtbl	Purl 2 stitches together for a single left-leaning decrease by inserting right needle into back loops of 2 stitches at once and purling them together as 1 stitch. 1 stitch decrease.
partial	You do not work a full round, but instead stop short of end as indicated to work only a partial round.
PM	Place marker
PMW/X/Y/Z	Place marker W/X/Y/Z.
prep	Preparatory
psplitA&B	Using Yarn A&B held together, purl into the Yarn A and Yarn B sections of next stitch individually, as if they were 2 separate stitches. 1-st increase.
psso	Pass slipped stitch(es) over.
pwise	Purlwise
RLI	Right-leaning lifted increase. Work a stitch into the right shoulder of the stitch in the row below of the next stitch. 1-stitch increased.
RS	Right side
sk2po	Double decrease with dominant side stitches; Slip 1 stitch knitwise, knit next 2 stitches together, pass slipped stitch over. 2-stitch decrease.
sl	Slip stitch
SM	Slip marker
SMW/X/Y/Z	Slip marker W/X/Y/Z
splitA&B	Using Yarn A&B held together, knit into the Yarn A and Yarn B sections of next stitch individually, as if they were 2 separate stitches. 1-st increase.
ssk	Slip slip knit for a single left-leaning decrease by slipping 2 stitches knitwise, returning them to the left needle and knitting them together as 1 stitch through the back loop. 1-stitch decrease.

ssp	Slip slip purl for a single left-leaning decrease (right leaning on front) by slipping 2 stitches knitwise, returning them to the left needle and purling them together as 1 stitch through the back loop. 1-stitch decrease.
st(s)	Stitch(es)
UK	United Kingdom
US/A	United States/of America
WS	Wrong side
w&t	Wrap and turn; after working the directed number of stitches move the yarn to the other side of the work, slip the next stitch, move the yarn back to working position (to wrap the stitch), put the slipped (and now wrapped) stitch back on to the left needle, turn the work around and knit or purl back to where indicated. This creates a short row.
yds	Yards
yo	Yarn over. 1-stitch increase.

community pages.

This book is infused with the knowledge and support of many, both those named for their very specific contributions and others behind the scenes. None of us knit (create, write or live) in a vacuum and our skills are gathered over the years from those who teach us directly and what we glean ourselves by observing and otherwise experiencing what exists in the world.
I wish there were a way to highlight the tidbits of knowledge and expertise that have entered these pages via specific people, but that would become unwieldy and so, I shall take this opportunity to thank these wonderful people who made this book possible.

yarns.

The yarns used in this book were chosen for their quality and provenance, and equally because the people behind them make a big difference in their local knitting communities and beyond. For the most part, you buy these yarns directly through the producers or from an independent yarn shop. This way, the support stays where it's most valued with shepherds, spinners, dyers, knitters and your LYS. Here's how to find them:

Baa Ram Ewe www.baaramewe.co.uk
The Birlinn Yarn Company www.birlinnyarn.co.uk
Circus Tonic Handmade
www.etsy.com/shop/CircusTonicHandmade
Dandelion Yarns www.dandelionyarns.se
Daughter of a Shepherd www.daughterofashepherd.com
Ginger's Hand Dyed www.gingertwiststudios.com
Jill Draper Makes Stuff
www.etsy.com/shop/jilldrapermakesstuff
John Arbon Textiles www.jarbon.com
The Little Grey Sheep www.thelittlegreysheep.co.uk
Moeke www.moeke-yarns.com
Ovis Et Cetera www.etsy.com/shop/Ovisetcetera
De Rerum Natura www.dererumnatura.fr
Retrosaria www.retrosaria.rosapomar.com
Rosedean Ryeland www.rosedeanryelands.co.uk
Rusty Ferret www.fluph.co.uk
South Downs Yarn www.southdownsyarn.co.uk
Town End Yarns www.town-end-alpacas.co.uk
Valgaudemar www.filatureduvalgaudemar.com
A Verb For Keeping Warm www.averbforkeepingwarm.com
Viola www.violaandthemoon.com
Whistlebare www.whistlebare.co.uk
The Wool Kitchen
www.etsy.com/shop/Thewoolkitchen

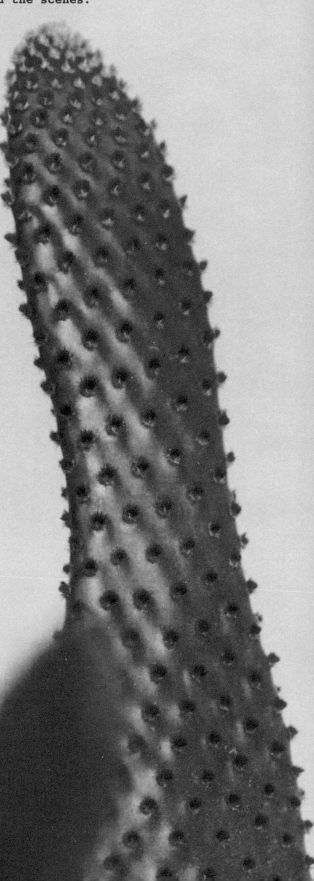

pattern testers and advisors.

I am indebted to the knitting friends who rigorously tested these patterns with generosity, patience, skill and enthusiasm. Not one of these patterns isn't five times improved because of their insights. There was a communal thrill of working together that falls into the exclusive, you-just-had-to-be-there category, but our behind-closed-doors collaboration has also improved these patterns no end for the wider community who will knit them next. We came at it with a good range of knitting experience, from the more timid, colourwork newbie to the confident, adventurous stalwart.

As all these patterns appear only in English, it felt important that they were tested largely by those who grew up speaking other languages. Excitingly, these included Cantonese, Danish, Dutch, Finnish, Flemish, French, German, Italian and Swedish. Dyslexic friends kindly tested the written instructions without the pictures of finished items they usually work from, knowing that by stepping out of their comfort zone, they would help others in the same position. Some knitted one pattern, others knitted multiple ones. I am grateful to them all. Here they are, in alphabetical order.

Jaclyn Beckner
Jenny Berman
Kristin Blom
Charlotte Bonduel
Jill Bulgan
Ceridwen Davies
Mariëtte van der Ent
Marie Eriksson
Emilie Fauerskov
Saskia de Feijter
Eva Fornazaric
Celine Gauthier
Maaike van Geijn
Josefine Hedlund
Johanna Höglin
Loveina Khans
Emma Kylmälä
Marie Lindblad
Madelene Linderstam
Jane Lithgow
Saskia Maas
Arijeta Makolli
Mimi McGarry
Joy McMillan
Ellie O'Rourke
Karen O'Rourke
Lina Ottemark
Yvonne Philippa
Helen Reed
Jeni Reid
Daphne Ruben
Sandra van Scheijndel
Ines Schweiger
Ellen Shek
Louise Spong
Anna Strandberg
Louisa Stratton
Cinthia Vallet

sample knitters.

As well as knitting all the patterns myself at least once, it was amazing to share the work of making samples with precise and skilled knitters. They saved my joints and my sanity. These are the surrogate knitters, who helped birth the samples you see on these pages:

Mandy Hewett
Emma Kylmälä
Pien Maltz-Klaar
Debbie Muir
Rachel Rawlins
Vonnie Williams

photography.

Elle Benton does it again! After *Penguin: A Knit Collection*, it was hard to imagine working with anyone else. She has an amazing eye and creative flair for finding stories between the knits and location, as well as a knack for working with regular folks, aka non-professional models. As in, she made us feel comfortable as well as look good. We share an affinity for colour and playfulness that she has the skills to capture in images. www.yellowbirdphotography.co.uk

models.

In order of apperance below:
Vonnie Williams
Marilla Walker
Anna Maltz
Adam Rompel

london locations.

The cactus lives on the gangway of our apartment building, a location you might recognise from *Penguin: A Knit Collection*. This adds a note of satisfying continuity, but is also as a reminder that what's right on the doorstep is enough! The tumbling blocks mural can be found in St Leonard's churchyard. The animal mosaics are in the playground on Hackney Downs. The floral mosaic is on the exterior wall of Columbia Primary School on Ezra Street, where you'll also find the dark-green door and pale-blue painted slats. All of these are in Hackney. The other photographs are taken in and around Brixton Market in Lambeth.

make-up.

Known more for adding colour to yarn as The Wool Kitchen, **Helen Reed** drew on her years of experience as a cosmetologist to add a little colour to our faces — just enough to make it easier to take the pictures (by stopping light bouncing off shiny noses and give a smidgen of shaping). And a little purely for the fun of playing dress-up.

editing.

A project of this scale and depth will inevitably have some errors and omissions. There would have been at least a million more if it were not for the keen eyes, wisdom and generous smarts of these women.

TECH EDITING
Rosee Woodland www.roseewoodland.com

COPY EDITING
Amelia Hodsdon www.woollenwords.net

EDITING SUPPORT
Saskia Maltz

Rachel Rawlins

Daphne Ruben

you.

What happens with Marlisle next will encompass an even larger community that includes you. I can't wait to see where it all goes from here.

The charted and written patterns in this book can easily be applied to other projects. In that sense, this is a stitch dictionary too (albeit an abridged one). The sections of guidance around and within the patterns themselves are also intended to be informative for those who might wish to create their own designs (without needing to start from scratch) to take Marlisle forward. You are most welcome and encouraged to use the term Marlisle for your own original designs using this technique.

I hope you will share your projects from this book (and your own Marlise designs) on social media using the hashtags provided in each pattern and #marlisle in general, so we can all easily find and admire them. If you get a comment or like from @sweaterspotter, that's me. There's a sweaterspotters group on Ravelry, where you can go to chat about your knits. You can find details of when and where I am next giving a Marlisle workshop and sign up for my mailing list on my website, **www.annamaltz.com**.

And finally, **thank you** for buying this book. I hope you enjoy your Marlisle adventure.

book design & right-hand woman.

Kristin Blom is my all round collaborator. Yet again, this book is her project too: we've worked on it together in so many ways, it's hard to know where to start. She's pattern tested, kept things on track with deadlines and consistently offered unfailing honesty and support. When it comes to book layout, even when working with communications and as a designer, it takes a knitter to know what knitters need to make patterns a pleasure to follow on paper.

@LadyRowena on Instagram and Ravelry

life support.

A few people require a mention here, to acknowledge their unwavering support (because they're not already mentioned quite enough elsewhere in these Community Pages).

Tom van Deijnen
Saskia de Feijter
Anna Feldman
Felicity Ford
Bob Maltz
Pien Maltz-Klaar
Saskia Maltz
Adam Rompel

sewing patterns:
marilla walker.

Marilla Walker and I have a mutual appreciation of each others' patterns and approach to creativity and sharing. It made perfect sense to work together so that this book could offer you even more opportunity for your own creativity. The majority of the non-knitted clothes in the photographs are designed, dyed and sewn by her, meaning that you can make them too, because she makes patterns for the DIY sewer.

Marilla Walker
www.etsy.com/shop/MarillaWalker

These are the Marilla Walker patterns that are pictured:

Honetone Coat
Used to sew the red, mint, denim, beige and pink coats seen throughout the book.

Isca Dress
Used to sew the yellow, pink and orange and grey splatter-dyed dresses seen throughout the book and the chambray one too.

Maya Top
Used to sew the tops worn by Vonnie and Anna with the Selbbob Hat (page 124).

Only a few other garments appear and these are 'models' own' (ie shoes, jeans, tights and Adam's peacoat and red shirt).

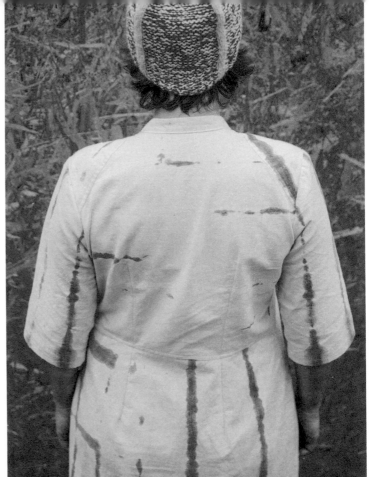